How to be a better writer online overnight

By
Richard E. Rotman

February 2019

Table of Contents

For the incredibly supportive Ellen, the love of my life, and Josh and Tal, the greatest son and daughter you could possibly imagine – and all the people who have allowed me to improve their writing.

A billboard in the wilderness is like a tree falling in the forest. Does anyone know it's there? How can anyone find it?

INTRODUCTION

Search engine optimization and earned media have become a content provider's most important skills. From a business perspective, get search right, and you connect with that most wonderful thing of all, a new customer. Get it wrong, and the potential customer will locate the competition and your market share and business will suffer.

However, writing for social media like Instagram, Facebook or Twitter or websites or blogs must be short and concise. It's intended for reading on phones and tablets and even smaller media like wearables. Too often it is full of excess verbiage. The ultimate goal, reducing word and space count while retaining the same meaning, cannot be ignored. No one but no one, wants to read big online copy blocks. It is such a turnoff.

How to be a Better Online Writer Overnight makes a bold claim, improving your writing in one day. It sounds audacious but it's true. Once applied, this writing system immediately improves almost any sentence, and shortens paragraphs and documents by 20-30 per cent while maintaining the same meaning. Apply it and there will be clearer, more concise paragraphs with fewer words; mistakes will quickly disappear. And all you need to do to start is learn three words: Of Is and By!

It's simple, it's basic and it works. The technique has been applied and refined among thousands of college and university students, and at major international communications firms. The changes are quick and dramatic. And yes, it will happen overnight. I mean it.

Who can benefit?

For people whose career involves online content writing or journalism, information must be conveyed concisely. Writing with flair and style then becomes the key to career success in PR, advertising, marketing, social media, websites, blogs, journalism and internal and external communications. As a result, it can attract positive attention from supervisors and managers who recommend promotions and salary increases.

With *How to be a better writer* at your side, this can be you.

This book can help you understand how to think differently, when it comes to your content. It will make a huge difference in your career as a content creator, helping your bosses and supervisors stand up and notice their search ranking climb up and up.

How it works

The book's main purpose is to compress and reduce words, while maintaining the same meaning. Each section contains actual examples of sentences drawn from university student papers, writing seminar participants and publicly available PR newswires. They all benefit from editing. The fix that's applied is explained, with the word reduction indicated. There are specific reasons describing what was done and why. Exercises (and answers) help you to apply the lessons just learned. There is a section with additional writing tips, based on the most common mistakes. Most people have a specific range of repeated writing problems. Identify and eliminate them -- and writing improves. This book helps readers find problems and quickly perfect their writing, while continuing to explore other difficulties.

There are six sections to the book:

1. Supercharge your writing skills with three two letter words: *OF IS and BY*
2. The 15 best writing trips
3. The better writer in action: actual news stories, edits and comments
4. Putting it all together with exercises
5. The 10 best PR Tools – a career reflection
6. Additional readings

At its most basic, *Better Writer* shortens sentences, eliminating words as follows:

OF

The pride of America, the pride of Canada. (8 words)

America's pride, Canada's pride. (4 words).

IS

Susan is the best person for the job, and she starts Monday. 12 words

Susan, the best person for the job, starts Monday. (9 words)

BY

The ball was thrown by John. (6 words)

John threw the ball. (4 words)

The chapters will help you master these concepts and employ them in your own content. Good luck!

Section I:
Supercharge Your Writing Skills With These Three Words

Chapter 1

HOW TO ELIMINATE 'OF'

Essential lesson #1 Start to use apostrophes instead of 'of'

English has a punctuation mark—the apostrophe—almost un-known in other languages. It forms a possessive. This mark is everywhere. Joe's Place. McDonald's. Tom's, Fred's, Sarah's. To start improving your writing immediately, every time you view the word 'of' in a sentence ask yourself if it can be eliminated. Use global search to find 'of.' It can't always be expunged so it's something of a trial and error process, as is all good writing.

In the next sections, there will be an original sentence A and the edit B, with the rationale for the changes outlined.

A. Beth Potter is the president and CEO of the Tourism Industry Association of Illinois, and she spoke first. (18 words)

B. Illinois Tourist Association CEO Beth Potter spoke first. (8 words)

What to observe: first, note in the sentence that there are two 'ofs' – 'of the Tourism Industry' and 'of Illinois' -- and those con-stitute word repeats, too. As 'is' will be this book's second major lesson, note that it is there too. 'Beth Potter is...'

Let's break it down

Beth Potter is the president and CEO

- Immediately 'is' makes Of Is and By editing pencils twitch. Use the comma instead of is: Beth Potter, president and CEO...

- Titles can almost always be compressed; are both necessary?

- Beth is the CEO, the top job; must she also be identified externally as president? We could write: CEO Beth Potter.

Then let's say that the group's official name is the Tourist Association of Illinois. Is it absolutely required in copy? Could it be shortened?

How about: Illinois Tourist Association?

Put it all together and you get:

Illinois Tourist Association CEO Beth Potter spoke first.

The next example

A. Fedeli served as <u>mayor of the City of North Bay</u> for seven years before representing the city in Albany. (19 words)

B. Fedeli served as North Bay's mayor for seven years before representing Nipissing in Albany. 14 words

How to fix it?

Let's start with:

Mayor of *the City* of North Bay

What do we notice?

Words to eliminate: 'Of the city...of North Bay.'

Change to: North Bay's Mayor.

Where do we put 'the city' of North Bay?

North Bay is by implication a city, especially because 'mayor' points us in that direction. Governmental distinctions are almost never necessary. Can we say:

North Bay Mayor?

Yes, we can.

Chapter 2

LET'S GET RID OF 'IS'

Essential Lesson #2 Now that we've eliminated of, let's look at 'is.'
It's the second word that improves writing immediately.

Many languages function admirably without 'is' in the present tense. In Russian, one says "I Moscow person," and it's the same in Hebrew and Ebonics (Black American English). Here's how to find this mistake easily:

Original and edit

- IDS is located in Toronto and has helped to improve the design scene in the city. (17 words)

- Toronto's IDS has helped to improve the city's design scene. (11 words), an almost 45 per cent reduction

A perfectly understandable sentence, grammatically correct -- and yet it can be improved radically.

The first concept to master: use commas to eliminate 'is.' Technically, this is called an 'appositive clause,' which provides additional information about a noun.

Start with the sentence's beginning:

- IDS is located in Toronto becomes
- IDS, located in Toronto...

Strictly speaking, located in Toronto is also redundant can be eliminated (this will also be covered later).

Change to:

- "Toronto's IDS"
- Now we add the second part:
    - Toronto's IDS has helped improve the design scene...
    - This also eliminates another word: 'and,' always a good goal. Then there is 'in the city.' Do we need that? Watch this:
    - Has improved the design scene in the city
    Becomes:
    - Has improved the city's design scene.

Put it all together and again you get:

Toronto's IDS has helped to improve the city's design scene.

Let's try another sentence with 'is.' The questionable parts are underlined.

Original and edit

A. Kaling is well known for <u>her work on</u> the hit television series *The Office* and <u>is</u> also the star <u>of</u> her own television series *The Mindy Project*. (27 words)

B. Kaling, well known for the hit television series The Office, also stars in The Mindy Project. (17 words)

Commentary

- Both usages of 'is' have been eliminated.

- Kaling is well known for <u>her work on</u>...becomes -- Kaling, well known for the hit television series *The Office*...the comma clause saves the day.

- If television is introduced, series does not have to be mentioned twice.

- As they are in the same sentence, The Mindy Project can be assumed to be on TV and not a movie.

- Avoid repeating the same word twice in a sentence...use 'series' and then 'show.'

- Saying 'for her work' doesn't add much, as she is known for the series in which she does work.

The phrase 'is also the star of' is made much stronger by moving right to the verb: "also stars." This edit also eliminates the 'of' and makes it fewer words.

And the end result is again:

Kaling, well known for the hit television series The Office, also stars in The Mindy Project.

Alternate version

Well known for the hit television series The Office, Kaling stars in The Mindy Project.

I favor constructions like these.

By starting with "well known" and moving Kaling to the next part of the sentence, the first clause introduces the less important part and the subject is made closer to the verb.

Note how removing the 'is' changes the sentence. The verb then can become more active.

We removed the 'with' and moved up the verb's location changing it from 'showcasing' to 'showcases,' much more active.

Essential tip #1: not everything must be spelled out. Kaling being on a TV series implies work; is also the star of her own series can easily be shortened. If it's named after her, then it's her own series.

EXERCISES

- The city's newest museum is the first dedicated to Philadelphia's modern history, with artifacts and exhibitions showcasing the <u>1920's</u> to the present. (23 words)

- The city's newest museum, the first dedicated to Philadelphia's modern history, showcases artifacts and exhibitions from the 1920s to the present. (22 words)

Commentary

- The gentle reader might ask why it's worth editing to get rid of just one word—23 words vs. 22?

- The answer: readability.

- The second example is easier to read. It's more active— 'with artifacts and exhibitions showcasing...' changed to 'showcases artifacts and exhibitions,' an active voice.

- Writing tip: it's 1920s, no comma, not 1920's; that's a possessive.

Now try this:

A. The Hospital for Sick Children is extremely <u>lucky to have so many generous</u> and dedicated supporters. The compassion of our supporters is what allows the hospital <u>to do so many great things for the children across the continent.</u> (39 words).

B. The Hospital for Sick Children's many generous and dedicated supporters allow the hospital to accomplish a great deal for the continent's children. They fortunately help achieve our goals. (28 words).

Commentary

- Take a look at how The Hospital... is extremely <u>lucky to have so many generous</u> becomes 'The Hospital's...many generous and dedicated supporters.
  - Much more active and stronger, and the 'luck' factor can be conveyed elsewhere.
- Of course, when there is an 'is', that's an immediate sign to reconsider a phrase.
  - Then there is a word repeat, always a danger sign.
- The compassion of our <u>supporters</u>-- Dedicated supporters.
  - Word repeats occur not only in the same sentence but also in nearby ones.
  - Using 'supporters' in the first part covers it adequately.
- To do so many great things -- accomplish a great deal...use stronger verbs over ones like 'to do, to get and to have.'
- For the children across the continent -- for the continent's children. There need not be an 'of' to take advantage of the glorious apostrophe.

Additional fixes

Original

A. Green Events is our team of talented event producers, <u>who work tirelessly</u> to get brands face to face with their target audience through creative intelligent events both locally and internationally. (30 words)

B. Our talented Green Events producers work tirelessly to place brands in front of their target audience locally and internationally through creative intelligent experiences. (23 words).

Commentary

• By making 'our talented...producers' the subject, the 'is our team of talent producers' rids the sentence of the 'is' and paves the way for deleting 'who work.'

• The much simpler construction, 'producers work tirelessly,' makes the sentence stronger and shorter.

Original

A. Efficient communications is critical in the construction industry and having the ability to quickly connect <u>multiple</u> people, groups and jobs sites are key to keeping a project on-time an on-budget. (30 words)

B. Efficient communications, critical in the construction industry, offers the ability to quickly connect people, groups and jobsites -- the key to keeping a project on-time and on-budget. (27 words)

Commentary

- The appositive clause again saved this sentence, transforming 'is critical' into a clause followed by a verb: 'offers.'
- It's not that much shorter but any reduction is worthwhile.
- 'Multiple people' is an interesting one.
- People is a plural so 'multiple' can be removed.

Original

A. Staying connected with mobile and stationary <u>workers is critical</u> for ensuring employee safety, improving productivity, reducing costs, and growing revenues. PTT is fully integrated and hosted in the company's secure networks <u>so we</u> can provide reliable, instantaneous communications. (38 words)

B. Staying connected with mobile and stationary workers ensures critical employee safety, improves productivity, reduces costs, and grows revenues. PTT, fully integrated and hosted in the company's secure networks, provides reliable, instantaneous communications. (31 words)

Commentary

- Two uses of 'is,' and a 'we' are eliminated, and it means the very same thing.
- Is critical for ensuring employee safety becomes 'ensures critical employee safety.'
- Note how 'is critical for' is wiped out when 'critical' moves to modify employee, and also carries the same meaning.

Original

A. With the largest LTE network, your business is covered from coast to coast. <u>We also work</u> with a robust network

IoT partners and hardware providers to meet your unique business needs. (31 words)

B. The largest LTE network covers your business from coast to coast, working with robust network IoT partners and hardware providers to meet unique business needs. (25 words)

Commentary

- 'Covers your business' is far stronger than 'your business is covered,' with an active voice employed.

- And the bonus: eliminating 'we also work' with 'working with,' an example of using a gerund (ing) to shorten sentences. (See later chapter on this).

More edits to review

A. Verizon is only 1 of 2 providers to offer the quality and service level only carrier-grade PTT can provide. (20 words)

B. Verizon, only one of two providers offering the quality and service level only carrier-grade PTT can provide. (18 words)

C. Verizon Push-to-talk is an end-to-end communications solution that allows for instant voice communication with one person or a group of people. 22 words

D. Verizon Push-to-talk, an end-to-end communications solution, allows instant voice communication with one person or a group. (17 words)

Essential Tip #2: Eliminating of and is launches the battle but seeking out other words that can be modifiers like 'in the state'-- 'the state's and 'we have discovered' -- without prevention' is the second stage in the war against excessive verbiage.

Chapter 3

BY AND THE PASSIVE VOICE

Essential lesson #3: Find the word "by" in your content and eliminate it. Active writing is always better than passive. It also eliminates unnecessary words. If "by" follows a verb, it's a passive voice.

Writing gurus from E.B. White (The Elements of Style) to Ernest Hemingway suggest avoiding the passive voice. It is one of the most important and time-honoured writing tips.

At its simplest, it works as follows.

The pitch was thrown by Roger Clemens.

Becomes...

Roger Clemens threw the pitch.

Lawyers write with the passive voice; perhaps because it shows who did what to whom. Nobody ever held up lawyers as good writers. Their objective is not communications writing, which tries to keep it simple.

Not every "by" can be eliminated, especially in expressions of time or direction. "Be here by 9 a.m. -- or else! is not a passive voice. Neither is: "by the time you arrive" or "by the side of the road." Learn the difference.

Correct this:

A. Remarks by the minister

B. The Minister's remarks

Some examples:

Original

- The celebrated Corvette, <u>made by Chevrolet</u>, offers outstanding <u>value in a sports car</u>. (13 words)
- Chevrolet's celebrated Corvette offers outstanding sports car value. (8 words)

Commentary

- 'Made by Chevrolet' -- Chevrolet's. Use of apostrophe eliminates "made by."
- 'Value in a sports car' -- Outstanding sports car value.' Moving sports car in front of value eliminates "in a."
- While 'by' is the main focus, we will also find other ways to slim down our words, as we move through *Of Is and By*.
- The next sentence combines eliminating 'by' and 'of' so will help us work on both.

Try this pair and change the passive voices.

A. The amendment was <u>introduced by</u> the Democratic member of the Legislative Assembly of Wisconsin, France Gélinas. (17 words)

B. France Gélinas, Democratic member of Wisconsin's Legislative Assembly, introduced the amendment. (13 words)

Commentary

- 'The amendment was introduced by...' This should raise a red flag instantly. How can it be active?
  - Change it to: France Gélinas introduced the amendment.
    - That's more active
  - She, however, needs her titles and affiliation explained.
    - 'Of the Legislative Assembly of Wisconsin' – Wisconsin's Legislative Assembly
  - We reduced 17 words to 10, a big victory.

More exercises

Original

A. You are invited to attend the announcement <u>of the competition winners by</u> Mayor Tory. (14 words)

B. You are invited to attend Mayor Tory's competition winners' announcement. (10 words)

C. Please attend Mayor Tory's competition winners' announcement. (7 words) (an alternative, slightly less preferable)

Commentary

- The 'by' at the sentence's end sends an immediate danger signal.
  - Make it a possessive: Mayor Tory's.
- The same with 'of the competition winners.'
  - It, too, becomes a possessive.
- Even 'you are invited to attend' can be shortened to 'please attend.'

I love those kinds of reductions. Seeing 14 words become seven warms my little editor's heart.

Additional exercises

Remove the passive voices.

A. Councillor Anthony Perruzza put forth a motion to have a report done by General Manager, Transportation Services to his committee. It was seconded by Councillor Gary Crawford. (27 words)

B. Councillor Anthony Perruzza moved that the General Manager, Transportation Services report to his committee. Councillor Gary Crawford seconded the motion. (20 words)

Commentary

- In addition to the passive voice, there are many elements to change.
  - 'Put forth a motion to have' cries out for shortening.
  - 'Moved' does the trick and allows the subjunctive: 'moved that the General Manager…report."
- 'It was seconded by' — 'Crawford seconded the motion.'
  - Much better as an active voice, of course.

Eliminate the 'by' in these sentences. Also eliminate word repeats.

A. We offer end-to-end solutions that can be used <u>by</u> every industry. (12 words)

B. Every industry can use our end-to-end solutions. (8 words)

Combining the lessons

Now that you have learned Of Is and By basics, this section combines exercises and examples combining these three important tips.

More passive voices—try and edit

A. Before his *BOOM POLITIC* show <u>opens to the public</u>, <u>we'd like to invite you</u> to a unique bullet hole art performance by artist Viktor Mitic.

B. Before his *BOOM POLITIC* show opens, join us for artist Viktor Mitic's unique bullet hole art performance.

Commentary

- 'Join us' is shorter and more personal than 'we'd like to invite you to.'
  - 'Opens to the public' is easily changed to 'opens.'
- Who else would it open to if not the public? It's implied in 'opens.'
- Make the artist's name active with the possessive – Mitic's unique...performance

Of is and by; sentences with all three

Original

<u>The City of Toronto</u> turns into a night of <u>contemporary art with Nuit Blanche</u>. Nuit Blanche is an event held from sundown to sunset, this year <u>will be</u> the tenth edition <u>of</u> the contemporary art show. It will feature more than 110 projects <u>by</u> 400 artists. (46 words)

Edit

With Nuit Blanche held from sundown to sunset, Toronto turns into a contemporary art night. This year, the show's tenth edition, features more than 400 artists, and 110 projects. (29 words)

Commentary

- 'With Nuit Blanche held from sundown to sunset' – move to the beginning.
  - It sets up its identity immediately and then allows the descriptions to unfold.
- Nuit Blanche is an event held – the word 'event' is like 'city of.'
  - Clearly Nuit Blanche is an event, so delete that word and moving the timing 'sundown to sunset' up front makes the entire idea more concise.
- The City of Toronto – Toronto.
  - Use just the city; clearly Toronto is a city; it doesn't need a descriptor.
- Turns into a night of contemporary art -- Turns into a contemporary art night.
  - Art modifying 'night' works better and gets rid of the nasty 'of.'
- This year will be the tenth edition of the contemporary art show – 'Will be' is a disguised 'of.'
- Note how the comma clause, as is done with 'is' works here: 'This year, the show's tenth edition,' features, instead of 'it will feature more than 400 artists'; the future is implied and the passive 'by artists' is rendered into an active clause.

A great deal for one simple sentence!

A practice weighing down unsuccessful writing is burying the subject. Nuit Blanche is what's being written about and it's the cause of the city turning into an art gallery. The essential information is also its nighttime hours. The rest is filler. Note there is not one Of Is or By in the edited version.

A few more; correct the underlined parts.

Original

    A. The art show brings approximately 1 million people to the downtown core, including 200,000 <u>from out of the city</u>.

    B. The art show brings approximately one million people downtown, including 200,000 tourists.

Commentary

- Numbers under 10 are spelled out.
- 'From out of the city' is four words.
- 'Tourists' implies out of town visitors.
- 'The downtown core' can mean something specific but 'downtown' also covers it.

Original

    A. Artists <u>from around the world</u> take part in <u>Art Battle 308. Art Battle 308</u> is the epitome of arts and culture scene in Toronto.

    B. International Artists take part in Nuit Blanche's Art Battle 308, the epitome of Toronto's arts and culture scene.

Commentary

- 'From around the world' – international means the same, replacing four words with one.
- Avoid word repeats —Art Battle followed by Art Battle.

- There isn't a good reason for there to be two sentences.
- 'In Toronto -- easily becomes 'Toronto's.' Use those apostrophes, when encountering 'in' before a location.

Let's rewrite

Now you try the following sentences. They each present different 'Of Is and By' problems.

A. I will follow up <u>with you by telephone</u> next Monday September 15, <u>2017</u>.
B. I will follow up Monday September 15.

Commentary

- 'With you by telephone' is superfluous.
- Readers know they are being addressed and the type of follow up, with a telephone, drone or singing telegram is irrelevant, as long as it happens.
- A good rule is don't use the year—2017—if referring to the present.
- If it's next year, or the last use the year.
- I always eliminate the days along with the dates. One or the other.

Use the three words to shorten the following:

A. After the media conference, Dr. Kaplanis, <u>accompanied by</u> Centre Director Joan Finch, will <u>give a guided tour of the facility</u> as well as <u>a demonstration of the interactive</u> classrooms. 29 words

B. After the media conference, Centre Director Joan Finch accompanied Dr. Kaplanis in a guided facility tour as well as an interactive classroom demonstration. (23 words)

Commentary

- This sentence demonstrates interesting points, and not just the word reduction.
- 'Accompanied by Centre Director' – 'Centre Director Joan Finch accompanied'
- A guided tour of the facility' – 'guided facility tour'
- A demonstration of the interactive' -- 'interactive classroom demonstration
- Finally, in A., classrooms is correctly plural 'interactive classrooms' but in B., it's not.

That's English for you!

More exercises

A. The advance tour <u>of the</u> Bellwood's brewery will occur at 11 a.m.

B. The Bellwood's advance brewery tour occurs at 11 a.m.

C. The brewmaster will also lead a tour <u>of the</u> impressive facilities and guide you through a tasting of the twelve innovative taps and new food menu items.

D. The sportscaster once again shared the story <u>of</u> Walter Payton.

E. The sportscaster once again shared Walter Payton's story. *

*The Chicago Bear great; an NFL humanitarian award is named after him.

- Take out 'of' and 'the' drops away, too.

A. There is no way of knowing how much <u>of</u> the residual drug is left on any specific part of the patch.

B. Measuring how much residual drug is left on the patch is difficult.

Commentary

- 'Measuring' is more precise than 'no way of knowing?' It is subtle but it does eliminate letters and seems crisper—and this is a lesson in how to eliminate 'of.'
- As for 'how much of' vs. 'how much residual drug,' the answer is simple: we eliminate 'of' and 'the,' again making it more concise, and it means the same.
- When 'remains' replaced 'is left' two words became one and a stronger verb was used, which is always desirable.

A. The upcoming exhibition <u>at the AGO called</u> *Anatomically Correct* <u>is a group show of portraiture</u> photography on the issue <u>of body image</u>. (23 words)

B. The upcoming AGO group photography exhibition, *Anatomically Correct*, examines the body image issue. (14 words)

Commentary

- 'Upcoming exhibition' and 'Is a group show of'—both make the same point.
- At the AGO—move it before 'group.'
- 'Called' isn't necessary; use commas so 'anatomically correct' modifies 'exhibition.'
- 'Issue of body image' – Body image issue

A. I am confident that this conference will be <u>of</u> interest <u>to</u> The Globe and Mail as well as the anxious public.

B. This conference should interest The Globe and Mail as well as the anxious public.

- I am confident that or other phrases like it—I think that, etc.—are almost always superfluous and insert the writer into sentences unnecessarily.
- Note how 'will be of interest to' is easily replaced with 'should,' which brings in the writer's self-confidence.

A. Rick Ciccarelli a Boston-<u>based</u> researcher <u>was a part of the</u> Green Manufacturing Action Team and is chair of the Clean Trains Coalition.

B. The Green Manufacturing Action Team's Rick Ciccarelli, a Boston researcher, chairs the Clean Trains Coalition.

Commentary

- This pair has much to commend it as a learning exercise.
- To deploy an apostrophe, the 'Team' part was moved to begin the sentence.
- That identifies Ciccarelli as 'part of' the team.
- Calling him 'a Boston researcher' expunges the always extra 'Boston based.'
- Then, instead of 'is the chair of,' there's 'chairs,' a more active construction.

Exercises and commentary

In the following exercises, there is another *Of Is and By* concept that's outlined: excessive use of 'you' and 'your.' They can almost always be eliminated and the sentences below are an example.

Of (and your)
Original

A. We serve as the single point of contact to address all of your mobile needs including support and billing inquiries.

B. We serve as the single contact, addressing all mobile needs including support and billing.

Commentary

- Point of contact is a phrase like 'at this point in time' or 'on that day' that is easy to reduce.
- Change simply to 'contact.'
- 'All of your mobile needs' – 'all mobile needs'; they mean the same.
- 'Support and billing inquiries' – just 'support and billing'; the implication is that one would have to inquire to find out anything.

Original

A. Do not interrupt <u>a group of users if you need to reach</u> a single person.

B. Do not interrupt users to reach one person.

Commentary

- There really isn't a difference between 'a group of users' and 'users,' which are by definition a group.
- 'If you need to reach' becomes 'to reach,' implying the need in the first place.
- 'A single person' is the same as 'one' person.

Original

A. When <u>you need</u> the powerful capabilities <u>of a smartphone</u> to access to critical mobile applications <u>you get the speed of instant communication</u> to increase <u>your</u> productivity.

B. When a smartphone's powerful capabilities are needed to access critical mobile applications, combine them with instant communication to increase productivity.

Commentary

- While there are an equal number of words between 'you need' and 'are needed,' the latter is just more elegant and gets rid of 'you' again.
- Also moving it after 'smartphone' emphasizes the product.
- Next, 'of a smartphone' is a no-brainer: 'a smartphone's powerful capabilities' is so much stronger.
- By now the second 'of' should set off 'of is and by' alarms, and it does. 'Instant' implies speed, so it can be just 'with instant communication.'

Original

A. Take the complexity <u>out of</u> managing <u>your</u> mobile infrastructure and applications <u>in order to</u> free up <u>your</u> internal resources and stay focused on <u>your</u> core business.

B. Reduce complexity in managing mobile infrastructure and applications to free up internal resources and stay focused on your core business.

Commentary

- 'Take the complexity out of' – 'Reduce complexity in.' Fewer words!

- 'In order to' is something that can always be edited out. Not necessary. Just 'applications' to free up.
- 'To free up internal resources' removes the 'your' but 'your' works in 'your core business.' In these examples, four clauses with 'of' have been eliminated, with the surplus words accompanying them, and four 'you' and 'your' were eliminated.

Not all changes involve an apostrophe:

A. With a speech from CEO of MAC Cosmetics John Demsey
B. With a speech from Mac Cosmetics CEO John Demsey
   - Of is removed and CEO is placed before the name, always a good writing tip.

The great Argentine writer, Jorge Luis Borges, lamented the apostrophe's absence in Spanish, noting its absence added to the language's sonority—de la casa, de las montanas—but prevented the conciseness possible in English so we have it on no less the Nobel Prize winner's authority that this construction is a good thing.

BONUS QUESTION

Editing this sentence often bedevils students. Now that you are thoroughly steeped in at least the 'of' portion of "Of Is and By," try it. The edit is below, upside down.

A. Beth Wilson, Chair <u>of</u> the Board of Trade and managing partner of the Chicago office of KPMG, played an important role in the outcome. 25 words

Essential Lesson #1: Everyone including the author has certain mistakes made over and over. Excessive us of 'you' is one example.

These are words to find and trash. Use search to locate 'of' and 'you,' and then eliminate them wherever possible.

A. Beth Wilson, Board of Trade Chair and KPMG Chicago managing partner, played an important role in the outcome. 19 words

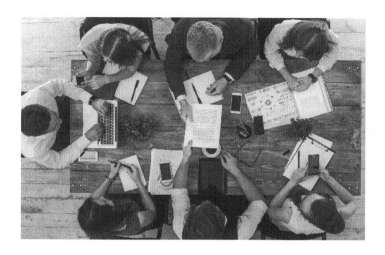

Chapter 4

HOW TO APPROACH EDITING YOUR OWN WORK

Now you've successfully mastered *Of Is and By*, a great achievement. Before turning to other writing tips, here is a checklist for editing sentences. It's my thought process.

Stage One

- Look for the words Of Is and By (obviously).
    - Can you use apostrophes instead of 'of?'
    - Introduce a comma clause instead of 'is?'
    - Are there passive voices where 'by' can be eliminated?
    - Are there word repeats? Even different forms of the same word or verb.
    - Can you find redundancies? Words like 'brutal murder' (all murders are brutal).

Stage Two (from section two)

- Is the sentence too long? Would a period between two parts help?
- Are there throwaway clauses? Words that are necessary but only add a detail in addition to the main point?
- Can you eliminate to for and on?
  - Discounts to Lululemon stores—Lululemon store discounts
  - The effect on the environment—environmental effect
  - Dependent on manufacturing—manufacturing dependent

Stage Three

- Is the 'it and they' reference correct? — institutions are it, people are they.
- Do the words 'located in' or 'headquartered in' exist in the sentence?
  - The crisis in Washington—the Washington crisis
  - Headquarters in New York – New York headquarters
- Is the meaning absolutely clear so that any reader will understand what you are saying?

Section II:
The 15 Best Writing Tips

Now that you've mastered Of Is and By, and reduced documents and sentences usually more than 20 per cent, there are many more easy ways to improve writing. In the following chapters, these tips will help move your writing to the next level. Combine them, and Of Is and By and you will quickly be a superstar. There are exercises and commentary and section illustrating how to improve just about any content but with a special focus on news releases, astonishingly distributed over paid newswires. The tips conclude with more individual examples, with more edits, exercises and commentary.

Chapter 5

Tip 1: to for and on

Due to English's flexibility, 'to for and on' can almost always be eliminated. At its most basic, here's how it works: "The effect on the environment" can be "environmental effect." "I gave the ball to John" can become "I gave John the ball." "The house on Main Street" can become "the Main Street House." It means exactly the same and is shorter, of course, and more compressed. Compress wherever possible.

Here are some examples:

FOR

Original and edit

A. The College becomes the first post-secondary institution to provide nap rooms <u>for</u> students, available 24/7. Rooms are located in L Building at Lakeshore campus <u>for</u> students.

B. The College becomes the first post-secondary institution to provide student nap rooms, available 24/7 in the Lakeshore campus' L Building.

Commentary

- In moving "student" to before "nap rooms," it eliminates the additional 'for' and means the same.
- The sentences were merged, with "students" cut in the second reference. "L Building at Lakeshore Campus" can easily be rendered as the "Lakeshore campus' L Building."
- This forgoes the more elaborate construction above and uses the possessive.

TO

Try this sentence

A. Unlike other yoga studios, memberships will include discounts to Lululemon stores, insight to new products, and free entrance to Lululemon events.

B. Unlike other yoga studios, memberships include Lululemon store discounts, new product insights, and free Lululemon events.

Commentary

- Memberships will include discounts to Lululemon stores – Change to: Memberships include Lululemon store discounts
- Insight to new products -- New product insights
- Free entrance to Lululemon events -- Free Lululemon events.

We've eliminated the word 'to' three times. It reads much better.

ON

On is similar to the 'to and for' descriptions. It can be replaced easily with the word it indicates becomes a modifier. Here are some examples:

Original and edit

A. In terms of location, Oregon is on the other side of the country, which provides more opportunity for awareness of Professor Rubin's new book.

B. Oregon, on the other side of the country, provides more opportunity for Professor Rubin's new book.

Breaking it down…

- In terms of location…this is one of those clauses that can almost always be edited out
  - Obviously Oregon is a location
- For 'of, is and by' devotees, the word "is" after Oregon should set off a red light.
  - "Is" must go.
- "Awareness of Rubin's new book" is the same as "more opportunity for Rubin's book."
  - Awareness equals opportunity.

Next example

Original and edit

A. Competition will be between oil-rich provinces and those who are dependent on manufacturing.

B. Competition will be between oil-rich and manufacturing-dependent provinces.

Commentary

- Both "oil-rich" and manufacturing dependent here refer to "provinces."
- Getting rid of "those who are dependent on manufacturing" eliminates five words, always a plus in good writing!

Essential lesson #2: Everyone has specific writing mistakes made repeatedly. The path to writing excellence means casting off these errors, once you identify them.

Chapter 6

Tip 2: don't confuse 'it and they'

Confusing 'it' and 'they' causes a fundamental mistake, confusing the difference between written and spoken speech. It also leads to verb and tense mistakes and is perhaps the number one writing error, which often distinguishes a professional writer from an amateur. It should be easy to catch but somehow, it's not.

Many things said are grammatically incorrect and would be out of place in writing and yet don't sound wrong in everyday speech.

You might hear a friend say: "Apple brought out the new iPhoneX and they are raking in the sales." However true, it's not grammatically correct.

Apple is an 'it.' Organizations, corporations and institutions take "it" in second references. People, descriptions of groups and plurals are 'they.' Harvard College launched its fall semester – not launched *their* fall semester. However, "Harvard students began their courses." Harvard and Yale Colleges issued *their* new curriculum.

Here are some examples:

Original and edit

A. Canoe restaurant is featured on the show, and *their* original award-winning chef, Anthony Walsh, will be preparing lunch. The table servers will be on *their* best behavior. Oliver & Bonacini will also be highlighting its many fine restaurants.

B. Canoe restaurant, featured on the show, will have <u>its</u> original award-winning chef, Anthony Walsh, preparing lunch.

Commentary

- Canoe is an 'it.'
- Servers are 'they' – their best behavior, as they are people.
- O&B operates many restaurants but is an organization
- O&B is an 'it.'

One more time – try it!

A. World-renowned Parisian bakery, Ladurée, will be launching <u>their</u> first New York location.

B. World-renowned Parisian bakery, Ladurée, will be launching <u>its</u> first New York location.

The tip: Just say it to yourself – it/organizations, they/people.

Essential lesson #3: When referring to corporations and organizations, following the name's first use, employ 'it' as a second reference.

Chapter 7

Tip 3: plurals eliminate gender bias

I shudder when in my predominately female PR writing classes, someone refers to "a student" as "he."

Fascinated with languages as I am, I muse over the idea that very few languages employ gender in the present tense but almost all do in the past. Remember your French with the verb changes when the antecedent is feminine. In Hebrew, interestingly, there is strict gender separation in the present tense, when saying I speak, a man says "ani mevin" and a woman "ani mevina." Thankfully, English has done away with most of that, though it once was as gender divided as its peers. Saying "she speaks, he speaks" makes sense when referring to someone specific.

Changing a singular to a plural does not change meaning; it eliminates gender problems and reduces awkward "he or she" constructions.

Examples

Original and edit

A. When I tell a student to turn in his or her paper on time, I want him or her to do so.
B. When I tell students to turn in their papers on time, I want them to do so.

Commentary

- "A student" to "students"
- "His or her paper" to "their papers"
- "I want him or her" to "I want them."

The benefits are clear, a shorter sentence and no gender bias.

This is certainly one everyone ought to adopt.

More examples

Original and edit

A. Have your child walk halfway up the slope and point the bike downhill. Have him or her coast down using their feet as brakes. (24 words)

B. Have children walk halfway up the slope and point bikes downhill. Have them coast down using feet to brake. (19 words)

Commentary

The meaning is identical, that's the beauty of plurals.

It also eliminates 'your', a pet peeve of mine.

Even with 'point the bike downhill' becoming 'point bikes downhill', plurals save that clause too without having a gender question at work.

'Have them' is so much better than 'Have him or her.'

So is 'using feet' instead of 'using their feet.'

Now you try

A. It's easy to look at a young politician and label him or her as too inexperienced or naïve.

B. It's easy to look at young politicians and label them as too inexperienced or naïve.

Commentary

Here the change to plural eliminated the need for 'a' young politician.

It was only shortened three words but there is a categorical difference in the sentence's effect.

Another

A. His or her new procedures are likely to clear up more confusion.

B. New procedures are likely to clear up more confusion.

Commentary

The 'his or her' is an immediate red flag. But look at how the sentence didn't need to be pluralized. His or her was superfluous copy.

A few more

- The presents were given to him and her.
- The presents were given to them.

A. He/She should be flexible, adaptable and results-driven, with the skills to work with stakeholders.

B. Individuals should be flexible, adaptable and results-driven, with the skills to work with stakeholders.

Commentary

- This was taken from a recruiting advertisement.
- Change the gender reference and it's even more politically correct.

Try this

A. The aim is to help his/her internal clients communicate with employees strategically and effectively so that client relationships are enhanced. (20 words)

B. The aim, helping their internal clients communicate with employees strategically and effectively, enhances client relationships. (15 words)

Commentary

- This combination demonstrates several important points.
- 'His and her' easily become 'their.'
- The second part solves an 'is' problem. 'The aim is' – 'The aim, helping...'
- Finally, the passive 'client relationships are enhanced' by virtue of the changes turns into the active 'enhances client relationships.'

Essential lesson #4: Plurals shorten sentences -- and solve gender problems. An egalitarian, progressive society, with equal opportunities for women, creates gender problems in masculine-based languages. This is one of the most important and innovative chapters in this book. Try and incorporate it into your writing immediately.

Chapter 8

Tip 4: eliminate 'in,' 'at' and 'located in'

1. Using "in" or "at" before locations is usually unnecessary.
2. Put the location before the noun.
3. Eliminate the word "location."

Some examples:

A. The company was located in Los Angeles
B. The Los Angeles company.
C. The hot dog in Chicago contains very specific ingredients.
D. The Chicago hot dog contains very specific ingredients.

(Steamed all beef Vienna hot dog and poppy seed bun with mustard, no ketchup, onions, pickle relish, a sliced pickle, hot pepper and celery salt--delicious!)

A. The bagel in New York, however, comes in many varieties. (Plain, poppy, garlic, rye, pumpernickel, etc).
B. The New York bagel, however, comes in many varieties.

This tip applies to more than food.

Politics

A. The crisis in Washington
B. The Washington crisis

Economics

A. The Euro will not replace the pound in Britain.
B. The Euro will not replace the British pound.

Location

Many beginning writers are dependent on the word "location" to describe places. This is, however, redundant.

A. Apple Inc., which is located (or based or headquartered) in Cupertino, will be introducing a new iPhone this fall.

B. Cupertino's Apple Inc.

Or as simple as:

A. My friend would like to find a good hotel located in Paris.
B. My friend would like to find a good Paris hotel.

All of the examples reduce words and increase clarity.

This applies to dates also. Take a look at this sentence:

Original and edit

A. Relations between Cuba and the U.S. have remained hostile since they were initially shattered with the Cuban Revolution in 1959, which eventually led to an embargo on imports from Cuba in 1960. (32 words)

B. Relations between Cuba and the U.S. have remained hostile since the 1959 Cuban Revolution initially shattered them; that led to the 1960 import embargo. (24 words)

Commentary

There are several points to consider

- The first is what is the sentence's subject?
- As written, it's as if it's 'between Cuba and the U.S.,' which would of course require 'has.'
- But it's not; it's relations, which requires 'have.'

Then look at this pair:

- Since they were initially shattered <u>with the Cuban Revolution in 1959</u>
  - Since the 1959 Cuban Revolution initially shattered them

Let's look then at dates. If you start to write a phrase with a date, see if the date can modify the subject it covers. Both dates can be moved.

A. With the Cuban Revolution in 1959
B. With the 1959 Cuban Revolution...
C. On <u>imports from Cuba in 1960</u>
D. That led to the 1960 Cuban import embargo (as a semi-colon clause).

Exercises

A. The performance will take place on Wednesday, June 17 at 10 a.m. <u>in the Moos Gallery located at</u> 622 Richmond Street West.
B. The performance will take place on Wednesday, June 17 at 10 a.m. in the Moos Gallery, 622 Richmond Street West.
C. He lives in an old home located on Main Street.
D. He lives in an old Main Street home.
E. On July 15 at 11:00 a.m., famous comedian Mindy Kaling will be on location at Indigo for a press conference about her upcoming novel, "Why Not Me?"
F. On July 15 at 11:00 a.m., famous comedian Mindy Kaling will hold a press conference at Indigo to discuss her upcoming novel, "Why Not Me?"

Essential lesson #5: turn locations into adjectives.

Chapter 9

Tip 5: the period is the writer's friend

Is there anything simpler? That little black dot at the end of a sentence. Full stop. Its role in good writing can be enormous as it separates the long, windy sentence from the shorter and more concise one.

To even think about the period, I owe the late *Washington Post* editor Richard Harwood a debt of gratitude. Legendarily tough Ex-Marine and wounded Iwo Jima veteran Harwood once slashed through my lengthy copy at the newspaper, shouting, "Put some f'in' periods in that." Then he pointed out how the judicious placement of a period caused much other non-essential copy to fall away. It's a small but influential lesson that remains during my entire writing life.

Imagine your sentence on a web page. A good way to conceptualize is several lines in an 8.5 x 11" page becomes six or seven online.

Tabloids like the New York Post or London Sun do this very well. Follow their concise and simple style.

Here is an example of what a Harwood period can do:

Original and Edit

    A. <u>The purpose of the bill is to reduce</u> the buying and selling of used fentanyl patches by implementing a patch-for-patch return policy <u>and in order for</u> patients to receive more patches they will have to return the same number <u>of used ones as were</u> issued to them. (50 words)

B. The bill's purpose, reducing buying and selling of used fentanyl patches, implements a patch-for-patch return policy. To receive more patches, patients will have to return the same amount issued to them. (32 words)

Commentary

- The purpose of the bill -- The bill's purpose. A classic of is and by-ism.
- Is to reduce -- reducing the buying and selling. In this we apply 'is' rules and add a gerund – reducing – and get rid of 'the buying and selling.'
- By implementing – a good example of when 'by' does not indicate a passive voice to edit.
- And in order for patients – two important points here.
  - 'And' often indicates a period should be applied.
  - 'In order to' can almost always be eliminated; very superfluous.
- The same number of used ones as were issued to them -- to return the same amount issued to them.
  - If they are being returned, they were likely to have been used, so 'used ones' not necessary and 'as were' is an unnecessary addition 'issued.'
  - Original and Edit

Use periods to fix this sentence and take care of the underlined parts.

A. Ontario's definition of cigarillos is similar to that in federal legislation, so that the legislation has little incremental impact over and above the federal level as it prohibits all filters, while federal legislation prohibits only "cigarette filters."

B. Ontario's cigarillo definition, similar to the federal one, displays little incremental impact over and above it. However, the provincial regulation prohibits all filters, while the federal one prohibits only "cigarette filters."

Commentary

- Definition of cigarillos -- cigarillo definition
- Is similar to that in federal legislation -- similar to the federal one.
  - Bracketed by commas, this demonstrates eliminating 'is' at its best.
- So that the legislation has -- has little incremental impact.
  - The comma clause permits moving right to the verb, changing has, a weak verb, to a stronger one, 'demonstrates.'
- Then the period comes to the rescue: the sentence stops at 'over and above it.'
  - Then, 'however' introduces the next part, which also eliminates the word repeat 'above the federal level' – 'federal legislation' with an 'it,' a very useful word.
  - 'The federal level' – Make it just 'federal.' By definition 'federal' is a level.
- *Essential lesson #6: If there are more than three lines in a sentence, find a way to break it up with a period. If it looks too long, then it is. Find a place to insert a period and good things happen.*

Chapter 10

Tip 6: its and it's are different

Because of the ease of making a typo rather than a grammatical error, this error appears a great deal. The rule is quite simple: its: possessive, it's: contraction. While contractions are not always recommended in formal writing, they have their place, in dialogue and less rigorous formats:

"It's a dog. It was its first bath."

Instructive New York Times headline (for use of its and it's)

On Immigration, Mr. Trump Shows Congress **It's** on **Its** Own

The essential lesson #7: Its is the possessive. It's is a contraction. Avoid this mistake.

Chapter 11

Tip 7: use stronger verbs

These include has, had, get, got, is, are, was and took and taken, among others.

English, with its French and Anglo-Saxon inheritance, offers a treasure chest of wonderful evocative verbs, so why use the weakest ones? This section again draws the distinction between written and spoken language. They are not the same.

Saying "I had a cold and she got me some chicken soup" indicates very little about a person's education or writing competence. Perfectly understandable, it might come out of a high school student or a PhD in English. Even so, it can be improved in writing.

Several possible versions.

    A. I was suffering from a cold and she made me chicken soup.
    B. Suffering from a cold, I was relieved when she made me chicken soup.

Some more examples.

Had

A. The museum had an exhibition of Picasso's works.
B. The museum mounted an exhibition of Picasso's works.

Has

A. He has a bad case of the flu.
B. He suffered from a bad flu. (Don't need 'a case of').'

Get

A. I get a dozen fresh eggs at the farmer's market each week.
B. I buy (or purchase) a dozen fresh eggs at the farmer's market each week.

Was (for more on "is," review Chapter II).

A. My father was in World War II
B. My father fought in World War II.

Taken

A. Now that the poll had been taken, the numbers were clear
B. Now that the poll had been tabulated, the numbers became clear.

Took

A. She took three carrots from the bunch
B. She picked three carrots from the bunch

- In this case, took is very neutral, where "picked" or "selected" implies a process of thought.
- It adds more to the sentence and puts the language at your command.

Essential lesson #8 – don't use weak verbs. Learn the auxiliary verbs and how to upgrade them to stronger, more expressive words.

Chapter 12

Tip 8: shorten could be able to, would be able to

With a nod to the great E.B. White in the Elements of Style, this essential lesson still applies: As White also said "brevity is the essence of style," this chapter will be short.

A few examples

A. He is able to hit the ball well
B. He can hit the ball well.

C. He would be able to show up
D. He can show up

E. He could be able to in a few hours
F. He can in a few hours.

Exercise - *you try it!* Correct this sentence...

A. Voters <u>are able to</u> cast their ballots between 8 a.m. and 8 p.m. when polls <u>will be able to</u> close.

B. (Voters can cast their ballots between 8 a.m. and 8 p.m. when polls close).

C. Note that 'when polls will close' changes to simply 'close.' By closing they must be able to close!

Essential lesson #9: If you write able to, would be able to, could be able to, shorten them to "can."

Chapter 13

Tip 9: avoid negative constructions

When the word 'not' appears in a sentence, try to eliminate it. Positive statements are more effective than negative ones.

This was a Hemingway favourite, as part of his desire to make language concise. A positive is always better than a negative. "I love you" is better than "I don't love you...anymore." Joseph Heller parodied this well in the anti-war classic, Catch 22, when he wrote, "The next thing Capt. Nately didn't do was..."

Examples

   A. Don't come late
   B. Arrive on time

   C. He did not enjoy asparagus
   D. He disliked asparagus

   E. She was not the first person who applied for the job
   F. She was the third person applying for the job

Essential lesson #9: Not is a warning sign for negative constructions

Chapter 14

Tip 10: Use adverbs

I like adverbs. Use them wherever possible. They eliminate extra words and strengthen sentences.

In the next example, note how 'in a positive manner,' can be reduced to one word – positively -- via an adverb, among other changes.

A. White Ribbon <u>engages</u> young men and boys <u>in a positive manner</u> to educate them on the challenges in language and behaviors, as well as harmful ideas of manhood that lead to violence against women. (34 words)

B. White Ribbon <u>educates</u> young men and boys <u>positively</u> on linguistic and behavioral challenges as well as harmful ideas of manhood leading to violence against women. (25 words)

Understanding the changes:

- The thoughts 'engages' and 'educates' can be combined because to educate is to engage.
- That moves educates to the first part of the sentence, shortening it.
- 'In a positive manner' becomes 'positively,' the stellar adverb at work.
- Instead of 'on the challenges in languages and behaviors,' I moved languages...in front of challenges, so it came out 'linguistic and behavioral challenges.'
- Finally, devoted readers will notice that I left in the 'harmful ideas of manhood' with its 'of'; 'harmful manhood ideas' just isn't as clear.

- And, finally, 'that lead to violence against women' easily can be compressed into 'leading to violence against women.'

Another example

A. It is clear that, while the public learns about the organization and the value for which it stands, online interaction is not successful.

B. **Clearly** while the public learns about the organization and **its value**, online interaction is not successful.

Commentary

- 'It is clear that' becomes 'clearly.' That's easy.
- 'And the value for which it stands' reduced to 'its value' is not so simple. While the previous construction is understandable, adding 'its' just cuts out the fat.

Exercises – correct this sentence!

A. The champagne was full of <u>bubbles</u>, it has affected her <u>with significant effect</u>.
B. (The bubbly champagne has affected her significantly).

- Full of bubbles – The bubbly champagne
- With significant effect (the noun) – affected (the verb) her significantly.

A. Her goals are lofty but achievable <u>in short order</u> and included the valedictorian <u>named each year</u>.
B. Her goals are lofty but achievable shortly and include the valedictorian named annually.

- In short order – shortly
- Named each year – annually

Essential lesson #10 Adverbs: use them. Once you get the hang of this, it will be second nature!

Chapter 15

Tip 11: Eliminate 'it' clauses

Example

(Presents several writing lessons).

A. <u>It's crucial</u> to keep your grill clean and ready for use <u>at a moment's notice</u>. Ensure you scrub your grill after each use. <u>It's easiest to</u> remove sauce and grease just after finishing.

B. Keep grills clean and ready for use. Scrub after cooking, removing sauce and grease immediately after finishing.

Commentary

- The command form---keep grills clean—implies 'crucial' so it can stand alone.
  - Changing 'keep your grill clean' to 'keep grills clean' uses the plural to shorten it.
- 'At a moment's notice' is implied in 'clean and ready for use.' The redundant words can be easily eliminated.
- The same logic applies to 'Ensure you scrub.'
  - Scrub is an imperative and embraces 'ensure.'
- Combining sentences with gerund/ing clauses also is a good technique and removes another 'it' clause 'removing sauce and grease.'
- And while we are at it, 'use,' repeated twice, was also removed.

Another

A. This summer <u>is predicted to be</u> hot and humid, <u>it's important to</u> be aware of a few tips to <u>stay</u> safe and healthy.

<u>It's important to stay</u> hydrated to not deplete your body from key nutrients or become at risk of heath stroke or heat exhaustion.

B. With a hot and humid summer <u>ahead</u>, stay safe and healthy by keeping hydrated; avoid depleting key nutrients <u>to prevent</u> heat stroke or exhaustion.

Commentary

- 'Is predicted to be' was removed in favour of 'ahead.'
  - 'With a hot and humid summer ahead' not only allows this but is more active.
- The imperative swings into action with the change from 'it's important to stay' to simply 'stay.'
- 'Avoid' also more concisely replaces 'to not deplete' and 'become at risk' is the same as 'prevent.'

One more

A. <u>Upon examination</u> of the 2014 Sony Entertainment Pictures (SPE) attack, <u>it can be determined that</u> cyber wars have advanced and <u>the amount of information</u> a hacker can obtain has substantially increased. (31 words)

B. The 2014 Sony Pictures Entertainment (SPE) attack determined that cyber wars have substantially increased the information a hacker can obtain. (20 words)

Commentary

- There is no particular reason to describe the examination process.
- Start with: The 2014 Sony Pictures Entertainment (SPE) attack determined...

- 'Amount of information' – just 'information,' please. It's the same.
- 'A hacker can obtain has substantially increased' is less forceful than 'have substantially increased the information.

Essential lesson #11 -- It clauses (it seems that…) are flabby, almost always unnecessary and use up space. Eliminate them by using imperatives or start with a verb. 'It' is a word like 'of is and by.' If you see it, get rid of it and make it positive.

Chapter 16

Tip 12: Avoid word repeats

I know how it works. We've all been there. Writers find a word and it fits, so it's repeated over and over, sometimes unconsciously. It's just in the mind while writing. These are word repetitions and are boring to read. They indicate the writer has not carefully reviewed sentences or tried to improve them. (Sometimes I will use U.S. and other times Canadian spelling. The U.S. is below).

Example

A. The <u>center</u> continually offers support programs, self-help tools and special events while inspiring and empowering those in need. The <u>center</u> includes one full-time employee and 50 volunteers. Prior to closing, programs were <u>run by paid</u> financial professionals. The center focuses on rebuilding operational structure since it reopened.

The changes, in two parts...

B. The center (*keep the first one*) continually offers support programs, self-help tools and special events while inspiring and empowering those in need. It (*instead of center*) includes one full-time employee and 50 volunteers.

C. Prior to closing, paid financial professionals operated (*stronger than run, and not passive*) <u>its</u> (*again, refers to center*) programs but now the focus after reopening is on rebuilding operational structure.

Important PR Writer tip: replace repeats with equivalents like 'it.'

Another

A. <u>Here you will have the</u> opportunity to cover the latest in <u>equestrian fashion</u> and apparel and discover what new and exciting things are on the horizon in the world of <u>equestrian fashion</u>.

B. There will be (*not you will have*) an opportunity to cover the latest in equestrian fashion (*keep this*) and apparel and discover what new and exciting things are on the horizon. (*The repeat is replaced by 'for it.'*)

Another with several tips

A. White Ribbon is a <u>male led</u> campaign to end <u>male's</u> violence against women. In 1991, a handful <u>of men</u> in Toronto decided they had a responsibility to speak against the Montreal massacre of the women engineering students just two years prior.

B. White Ribbon, a campaign to end violence against women, came about when some Toronto men made it their responsibility to speak out against the Montreal massacre of female engineering students two years prior.

C. Montreal's female engineering students massacre two years prior. (Eliminates 'of' but is inelegant. Here's where it's best to leave in the 'of.'

Commentary

- White Ribbon is a <u>male led</u> campaign to end <u>male's</u> violence against women.
    - White Ribbon, a male-led campaign...gets rid of 'is,' too.
- Often when eliminating 'is,' then it needs a verb to continue the thought, which is contained in the next phrase 'came about when some Toronto men made it their responsibility.'
    - In 1991, a handful <u>of men</u> – when some Toronto men...
- Understanding how to use 'it,' can be the simple key to eliminating repeats.

Another example

A. Although there are many wins within Canada's plan to reduce GHG emissions, <u>Canada</u> has maintained a "D" grade throughout the last two decades <u>on the</u> GHG emission report card

B. Although there are many wins within Canada's plan to reduce GHG emissions, it has maintained a "D" grade throughout the last two decades on GHG's emission report card. (*Even a way to get rid of 'on.'*)

Exercises – rewrite these sentences with word repeats and it clauses

A. The increase in digital media surely poses a threat to the print <u>media</u> landscape, however it offers opportunities for growth as well. With a digital society <u>that expects</u>

unlimited access to information, <u>it is imperative</u> that media operations adapt to societal demands for easily accessible online content.

B. The increase in digital <u>media</u> surely poses a threat to the print landscape. With a digital society <u>expecting</u> unlimited access to information, it must adapt to societal demands for easily accessible online content.

Commentary

- 'The print <u>media</u> landscape' – The 'print landscape,' or 'to print.'
  - 'Media' is unnecessary and a repeat.
- With a digital society <u>that expects</u> – 'expecting' makes it shorter and more active.
- <u>it is imperative that media</u> operations -- <u>media</u> must adapt.
  - With the it clause signpost, the notion of 'it is imperative' easily transmutes into 'must.'

One more

A. The College is <u>located</u> in Ward 6. Since 2003, <u>Councillor</u> Mark Grimes has represented the Ward and College <u>in city council</u>. Very few city <u>councillors</u> have the added responsibility <u>of</u> representing not only the residents of their ward, but also a major institution. 44 words

B. City Councillor Mark Grimes has represented Ward 6 since 2003. Very few have represented not only ward residents but also a major institution as an added responsibility.

Commentary

- This one is fairly straightforward. Reordering the sentence helped greatly.

- Moving the politician's name to the front allowed the next portions to be more active.
  - The word 'councillor' sets up the title so that in the next sentence, after 'very few' the title is implied and unnecessary.
- And because we are in the spirit of 'of is and by,' see how the last part was revised to get rid of the 'of.'
  - Instead of 'councillors have the added responsibility *of* representing not only the residents of their ward.'
  - Replace 'of their ward' by moving 'ward' to before 'residents,' so that it reads ward residents.

Essential lesson #12 -- If a word appears more than once in the same or adjacent sentences, change the repeated phrase. This is a simple method of ridding writing of noxious elements that drag down readability. Word repeats and it clauses often appear together. Edit out both!

Chapter 17

Tip 13: eliminate extra words

If this book's main principle is conveying the most amount of information with the fewest words—dynamically, and in the shortest time period—then this concept lays at the heart of the idea. If you can say things with fewer words, do it. To start with, there are a number of words and phrases that are often repeated and can almost always be eliminated.

One of the first is:

In order to

A. <u>In order for</u> this to be possible, the financial aid system must give additional assistance to post- secondary students <u>who are</u> underrepresented.

B. For this to be possible, the financial aid system must give additional assistance to <u>underrepresented</u> post-secondary students.

Commentary

- Truthfully, 'in order to (or for)' is rarely necessary.
- And always question whether clauses like 'who are' can be edited out. Slice those two words away and the fixes are simple:
- <u>In order to</u> ensure this, the organization fights to lower tuition fees – Change to: *<u>To ensure this</u>*, the organization fights to lower tuition fees.

Governments

Why younger writers persist in repeating governmental descriptors is beyond me. A city, state, province or country need not be identified as such.

The essential lesson:

When there is a modifier to a government, get rid of it. Some examples:

The city of Chicago

Chicago

The city of Toronto

Toronto

The state of Illinois

Illinois

The province of Ontario

Ontario

The country of France

France

Some examples:

A. Planned Parenthood Toronto (PPT) <u>is</u> a <u>not-for-profit organization</u>, which provides extensive community-based health care for <u>The City of</u> Toronto.

B. Planned Parenthood Toronto (PPT) provides extensive community-based health care for Toronto (or the city).

Commentary

A. This sentence not only has an 'is' problem but it also can excise the relative pronoun 'which.'

B. In general, describing something that's obviously a charity is only necessary when it's not clear.

News stories and articles

A. <u>A recent article in the</u> Washington Post highlights emerging health care issues stating that the District of Columbia ranks last <u>when it comes to</u> timely access.

B. The Washington Post highlighted emerging health care issues, stating that District of Columbia ranks last in timely access.

Essential tip: If it's a newspaper story, then it doesn't need to be described as an article. 'When it comes to' is superfluous; replace with 'in.'

Media, an unusual word.

Sometimes it's plural, sometimes singular. Classically and in Latin, it's a plural: medium, the singular, and media the plural.

Yet we say, "The media are here," or "The media is biased." Three ways to remember its usage:

- Referring to the news reporters: plural, the media are
- Referring to publications, broadcast outlets: singular, the media is
- Referring to works of art or one outlet: medium, 'she worked in encaustic,' or 'the medium is the message.'
  While we are on Latin, take a look at this mis-used word:
  - Alumnus – male singular
  - Alumna – feminine singular
  - Alumni – plural, men or mixed groups
  - Alumnae – feminine plural, women only

Essential lesson #13-- Eliminate extra words. It's different than word repeats.

Chapter 18

Tip 14: titles waste space

Titles, like president or managing director, suffer from excessive capitalization.

General rule: don't capitalize occupations but where someone belongs with their title, like a leader, then upper case the letter. President Obama, Prime Minister Trudeau. But GM president Fred Smith. Not Fred Smith, President of GM. Putting it before the title eliminates the 'of,' of course, which we all know by now.

Exercises

    A. Heather McGregor, CEO of the Dallas YWCA, will comment on the significance and impact of those contributions. 17 words

    B. Dallas YWCA

    C. CEO Heather McGregor, will comment on the contributions' significance and impact. 13 words

    D. Bruce Seeley, President and CEO of Multi Touch Digital Inc.

    E. Multi Touch Digital Inc. President and CEO Bruce Seeley

More title tips

- Use a person's given name along with their surname on first reference
  - John Tory, Kathleen Wynne
  - Don't use courtesy titles (i.e. **Mr., Mrs., Miss or Ms.**)
  - This rule does not apply to famous authors, composers and the like that can be referred to by surname only – Bach, Beethoven, Madonna

- Do not use false titles
  - Example: music pioneer Alanis Morissette
- Use titles on first reference, but seldom after that
  - Apple CEO Tim Cook
  - Cook
- Prime Minister Trudeau, President Barack Obama
  - Second reference: Trudeau, Obama

Courtesy and professional titles

- Use Dr. only for licensed health care professionals
  - Chiropractors, physicians, psychologists, dentists, veterinarians
  - But not on second reference – the last name only.
- Do not use Dr. for people with doctorates outside the health care field --Ph.Ds in PR or English, doctors of divinity (Maybe except for the Rev. Dr. Martin Luther King, Jr.)
- Use a religious title before a person's name on first reference
  - Father John McNally, Rabbi John Moscowitz
  - Subsequently, use the surname alone or the title preceded by the
  - The reverend, the rabbi
- Some religious leaders are known by their title and given name only (i.e. **Pope** Francis (no Roman numerals)
- The second reference can be either Francis or the Pope.
- Explain unfamiliar titles (i.e. **Primate** Michael Peers, the head of the Anglican Church)

The British Royal Family (and others)

- Members of the Royal Family in Britain
  - Prince and Princess before first names in the immediate Royal Family

- Prince Harry, Prince Charles (preferably The Prince of Wales)
- While their husbands are Prince William and Prince Harry, Kate and Meghan do not use the princess title although they could
  - The Duke and Duchess of Cambridge, first reference
  - The duchess, second reference
- Elizabeth, the reigning monarch in Canada: just the Queen
  - There is only one
- In the U.S., Queen Elizabeth II on first reference
- Her husband is Prince Philip, the Duke of Edinburgh
- Second reference: the duke (lower case)
- DO NOT use Sir...former Beatle Paul McCartney, not Sir Paul

Former titles are lower case

- Former president Bill Clinton
- Former prime minister Tony Blair

Essential lesson #14 -- Titles almost always waste space and can be compressed. Place them before the name.

Chapter 19

Tip 15: guide to most important punctuation marks

Among the most confusing and yet most important are colons, semi colons, commas, dashes and hyphens. Based on the most common misunderstandings among my writing students, here is a brief guide to those marks.

The Oxford comma

As this is being prepared for publication, the Oxford University Press has declared that commas are optional after a series: books, magazines and newspapers. Personally, I had thought that was not in conflict years ago. However, if the last item in the series is different than the first two then use a comma. As in:

Books, magazines, and trucks speeding down the street.

Colons

Colons are extremely useful. They introduce longer direct quotations and emphasize a series.

- Churchill said during the war: "This is not the end. It is not even the beginning of the end. But it is, perhaps, the end of the beginning."
- Highlights of Trump's speech: silliness, dishonesty, anger

They also take place of for example, namely, that is, i.e. in and amplification:

- It was a mixed cargo: iron ore, wheat and coal.
- Various solutions were considered: move to Canada, stay in the U.S., suffer Trump silently

Other colon uses

Do not capitalize first letter of sentence following a colon, unless emphasis is required.

They were relieved at the verdict: Not guilty!

Colons also create a strong contrast.

- Eating isn't just a necessity: it's an essential pleasure

In the case of titles and subtitles, they are essential.

- Trump: Portrait of a Scoundrel

In the Bible, chapters and verse are separated with colons.

- Proverbs 15:1

With all the stress on adopting modern North American style for quotes, colons are placed outside of closing quote marks.

- To the charge of "bigot": he said, "It's a lie."

Semi colons

Semi colons create a lesser stop than colons but are quite different. The clauses in a semi colon can stand alone but are linked. Using them avoids short choppy sentences and are a strong stylistic device.

- I love dining out; we go out often
- I wanted to go to Paris. She wanted to go too.
- I wanted to go to Paris; she wanted to go, too.

Combine sentences that would look too emphatic alone, combine them

- The man; the guitar; the blues.

Punctuation also is placed outside of quote marks.

Commas

They mark a series but not before the final 'and' unless the final part requires two words:

- Men, women and children.
- Breakfast was oatmeal, fried eggs, and bread and butter

Use commas in place of 'and'

- A frank, open face
- A well-meaning, enthusiastic student

Always place commas before conjunctions

- And, but, for or nor
- We are all in the gutter, but some of us are looking at the stars. – Oscar Wilde

Other comma tips

Use them to set off a long or short clause introducing the main idea:

- Even so, the vote was close.
- If God did not exist, it would be necessary to invent Him.

To set off parenthetical expressions, direct address etc. (but not etc.)

- Come here, Richard.
- Teaching is fun, isn't it?
- Your honour, I deny that.

With transition words, they provide a meaningful pause:

- Meanwhile, back at the ranch.

- In fact, I am right
- Of course, you are wrong.

Em dashes

An old printer's term, they derive from the length of the character itself. They can take place of commas, parentheses or colons. But use them sparingly, not more than two per sentence. Their most important use is enhancing readability instead of commas. They are less formal, more intrusive.

- After I got my car—three months after it was ordered—I didn't want it any more

To draw attention to content, use these em dashes as parentheses are considered more subtle:

- When the publisher saw the errors—125 of them—she withdrew the book
- When the publisher saw the errors (125 of them) she withdrew the book

Dashes emphasizes a conclusion:

- After months of deliberation, the jurors reached a verdict—guilty.
- White sand, ganja—this is why we went to Jamaica

(Note: without spaces on either side)

En dashes are smaller length, like an 'n.' Use them to span a range of numbers:

- 2016-2017 school year
- Chapters 8-12
- Office hours 8-10 a.m.

Scores and results also take an en dash, which is different than a hyphen:

- The White Sox lost 17-1, the House voted 365-1
- Conflict: liberal-conservative debate
- Connection: Toronto-Montreal flight.

Hyphens are not interchangeable with en dashes and are in fact a linking mark. They form compounds:

- eye-opener, check-in

They also modify adjectives:

- state-of-the-art projection

But don't use them after adverbs, a common mistake. Adverbs are independent (ly as an ending indicates adverbs).

- Poorly managed

Quotation marks Introduce or conclude a quote:

- "It was time to go," she said.

But leave off the comma if the quote is short and integral to the clause:

- Stop saying "I told you so."

Also introduce a complete sentence with direct quote:

- The prime minister replied, "I have nothing to add to what I said in the House."

Apostrophe madness

This important mark, so crucial to eliminating 'of' in this book also is used with verbs formed from capitals

- KO'd, MC'ing, DJ'ing, X'd out

Apostrophes also indicate plurals of lowercase letters

- Mind your p's and q's.
- Dot your i's and cross your t's.

But not with plurals of capitals or numbers:

- Straight As, (sometimes necessary: A's in writing and media relations)
- the ABCs, the dirty 30s

Also leave them off with common abbreviations:

- Cello, copter, flu, gym, phone (violincello, helicopter, influenza, gymnasium, telephone)

Essential lesson #15: The many English punctuation marks befuddle many writers. They are important, demonstrating skill and professionalism.

Chapter 20

MORE OF IS AND BY WRITING TIPS

Most writing mistakes are due to commonly made errors that writers make over and over again. Once identified, they can be pruned and edited. Here are some more tips. Some suggestions are for better writing; others cover grammatical errors that are not terrible but make writing look uninformed and less credible.

Flat adverbs, ones that don't end in "ly."

Don't use hyphens to form compounds with these words. They may look like adjectives but are actually adverbs and hence stand alone in a sentence. The catch is that some also contain the same form as adjectives and also can have 'ly' added in certain circumstances: hardly, lately, slowly and closely. Flat adverbs include:

- Hard
- Fast
- Little

- Well
- Late
- Very
- Almost
- Quite
- Just
- Too
- Far
- Slow
- Quick
- Straight
- Clean
- Fine
- Close

Hard-fought, fast-paced, little-known, well-prepared are not correct even if Word's spelling and grammar check identifies them as such.

Vary sentence structure

Too many sentences follow the same format. Noun verb object. They have clauses that could be turned around. In this sentence, note how the conventional structure is turned around.

A. Subprime mortgage holders pretty much managed their monthly payments as long as housing prices were jumping higher almost by the hour.
B. As long as housing prices were jumping higher almost by the hour, subprime mortgage holders could manage their monthly payments.

In the next example, there is what I call a 'throwaway' clause. Where the person lived or worked, is not as relevant as that it was 'deep and moving.' That's the thought to be left behind:

A. I've just returned from a very deep and moving experience living and working in Tel Aviv.
B. Living and working in Tel Aviv, I've just returned from a very deep and moving experience.

Neither are more correct. It just demonstrates the language's flexibility in that the sentence could be written either way to vary the reader's perception. Another way to accomplish this is to split sentences into smaller ones and then follow those by a longer phrase. Here are some more uses of the same concept, varying structure and applying some of the writing and punctuation tips above in what was written as a series:

A. Teens munching cucumbers on the bus as a "normal" snack
B. Teens "normal" snack: munching cucumbers on the bus

The colon eliminates many words and combines all the important ones.

A. Kids and adults in Purim costumes are <u>along the street</u> for days before Purim, all the while also attending lectures on the deeper meaning <u>of the holiday</u>
B. Kids and adults are walking outdoors in costumes for days before Purim, while also attending lectures on the holiday's deeper meaning

'Outdoors' is one word; 'along the street' is three. Of course 'of the holiday' becomes 'the holiday's.'

A. Walking to the synagogue on the Sabbath hearing "Shalom Aleichem" on the radio <u>coming out of windows</u>

B. Walking to the synagogue on the Sabbath hearing "Shalom Aleichem" broadcast on the radio

In this example, while it's true that the radio can be heard 'coming out of the windows,' it's almost as if the source is the windows. 'Broadcast' instead not only makes it clearer with fewer words.

A few more from the Holy Land:

A. The many Arab bus drivers we encountered on the public transport system
B. Encountering many Arab bus drivers on the public transport system

The bus drivers' identities are most important. Not who encountered them.

A. The two young Israeli soldiers on the bus fighting over who would give up his seat first for the elderly man just entering the bus
B. The two young Israeli soldiers fighting over being the first to give up their seats for the elderly man entering the bus

Only one reference to 'bus' is necessary, and the second example is just smoother, with the gerund clause...fighting over 'being the first.' Also two soldiers would take a plural — 'their seat.'

Who and Whom

These words are difficult and 'whom' can be avoided. In speech, 'whom' almost sounds pedantic; it is dropping out of general usage. In writing, however, incorrect usage is out of place.

Here is a simple definition:

- Who is a subject
- Whom is an object

'Whomever spilled stuff all over kitchen floor between stove and fridge should have cleaned it up' was one such message in our house. It's 'whoever,' as it's the subject. 'Whoever spilled stuff.'

If you can replace the word with "he'" or "'she," use who. If you can replace it with "him" or "her," use whom. Whom is used following words like to and for—to whom, for whom (the bell tolls)

- Him or her also substitutes for it, not he and she. Example "Whom will you invite?" (Will you invite him?)
- A good example of this is 'between you and I.' It should be 'between you and me.' The 'between' governs the 'me.' You wouldn't say 'between I and you.' But it's ok in speech; I no longer war against it as I once did, even though privately it still bothers me. 'It is I' is correct but people say 'It's me,'

Whose and Who's – a possessive pronoun vs. a contraction.

- Here we have a clear distinction that is also often messed up.
- There was a prize-winning play a few years ago called "Whose Life Is This Anyway." That was correct. "Who's here?" That's also correct.

Affect and effect is easier to learn than expected. Ways to remember which is which.

- Affect is a cause
- Effect is a result
- The affect of the effect

Think of that and you won't go wrong.

- Also affect is a verb and effect is a noun.
- "The net effect was to affect me."

In the next section, you will now see 'Of Is and By' in action, a section for communications writers of all sorts but especially relevant to PR, journalism and advertising/marketing. Hope this has been helpful so far.

Section III

THE BETTER WRITER IN ACTION: 15 NEWS RELEASES, EDITS AND REASONS FOR CHANGES

In this section, *How to be a better writer* will be put to work explaining edits to 15 publicly issued news releases. It will guide the reader through how to apply the book's tips, as if you were editing someone's copy. If you ever have anything to do with releasing information to internal and external audiences, this is for you. Professionals create, and organizations pay good money to release this news but don't bother to write it well. Why do they do that? Here are the originals with problem phrases underlined and suggested corrections, applying the Of Is and By system (and the other writing tips).

News Release #1

MCHAPPY DAY RAISES RECORD AMOUNT FOR RONALD MCDONALD HOUSES

In this story, the lead is confusing. It should really recapitulate and extend the headline. Instead the reader is diverted and shouldn't be. Start with the news: a fundraising record.

Original lead

Forty years ago, McDonald's Canada launched McHappy Day, the restaurant chain's largest one-day fundraising event of the year where $1 from every Big Mac® sandwich, Happy Meal® and hot McCafe® beverage sold is donated to Ronald McDonald House Charities®. This year marked the most successful campaign to date, with restaurants in BC and Yukon raising $530,849 dollars, a 40% increase from last year's raise. The funds will support the Ronald McDonald's House Charities network of programs in British Columbia, which supports thousands of families each year through its Ronald McDonald Houses and Ronald McDonald Family Rooms. (96 words)

Edit

In its 40th anniversary McHappy Day campaign, the most successful ever, McDonald's Canada franchisees in B.C. and Yukon raised $530,849 for Ronald McDonald House Charities®, a 40 per cent increase over last year. McHappy Day, the restaurant chain's largest one-day annual fundraising event, contributes $1 to the charity from the sale of every Big Mac®, Happy Meal® and hot McCafe®. McHappy Day supports thousands of B.C. families each year through Ronald McDonald Houses and their Family Rooms. (77 words)

Commentary

1. If it's the largest one-day fund raising event, it doesn't need 'of the year.' Annual is better and move it before 'one day,' as in largest annual one-day fundraising event.

2. Big Mac® sandwich, Happy Meal® and hot McCafe® beverage—do those terms really need identifiers; is there really anyone who doesn't know the Big Mac is a sandwich? And if those products need identification, why is the Happy Meal not explained? Make it Big Mac® Happy Meal® and hot McCafe®. Yours truly believes the ® mark is unnecessary, as publications never use it but here the lawyers no doubt sadly insisted on preserving it.

3. British Columbia references are inconsistent. BC is not publication style; B.C. is. If anything, first reference could be the full name with the second as B.C. Use 'per cent' not % in body copy. The $ implies dollars so do not say $530,849 dollars.

4. Word repeats should be avoided: 'raising' and 'raise' in one sentence; 'support' and 'supports'—that's just careless.

5. Ronald McDonald's House Charities is a lengthy first reference, and should be shortened and not repeated. Substitute 'the charity.' 'Ronald McDonald Houses and Ronald McDonald Family Rooms' can be 'Ronald McDonald Houses and their Family Rooms.'

News Release #2

AMERICANS BELIEVE REQUIRING PLAIN CIGARETTE PACKAGING WASTES GOVERNMENT RESOURCES UNNECESSARILY

Two passives in one lead, that's a record

This story, a major embarrassment, not only hides the sponsor's identity—a tobacco company—but it has a record two passive voices in the lead, and 44 words easily reduces to 36. The first research finding is pretty sloppy too, with three word repeats in one sentence. Shortening news releases isn't the only goal, making them clearer and more concise is just as important. In this example, the company made several grammatical, style and punctuation errors, in addition to employing clichés and failing to emphasize the most important thoughts.

Original

A new study <u>by Forum Research</u> shows consumers believe requiring plain packaging for cigarettes is an unnecessary waste of government resources. The <u>research</u>, commissioned by <u>JTI</u>*, comes at a time when people are concerned about the <u>regulation of controlled</u> substances. The <u>research</u> found that eight out of ten Americans (81%) believe that branding on <u>products</u> matters as it gives consumers information about a <u>product</u> and helps distinguish one <u>product</u> from another. 71 words

Edit

A new Forum Research study shows Americans believe requiring plain cigarette packaging wastes government resources unnecessarily, according to JTI-Macdonald Corp., which commissioned the study. As Americans are concerned about regulating controlled substances, the research found that eight out of ten Americans (81 per cent) believe that 'Branding on products matters as it gives consumers information and helps distinguish one from another.' 59 words

Commentary

1. *A new study by Forum Research* – Passive voice #1 becomes "A new Forum Research study." Not crazy about 'shows' but it does eliminate needing a 'that.'
2. *Plain packaging for cigarettes* – 'plain cigarette packaging.'
3. *About regulation of controlled substances* – 'about regulating controlled substances.'
4. *By JTI* – the full name is JTI-Macdonald Corp and it's Japan Tobacco's international tobacco division. It begs the question: who is JTI?

Comes at a time when Americans are concerned – 'As Americans are concerned.'

'**Branding on <u>products</u> matters** as it gives consumers information about a <u>product</u> and helps distinguish one <u>product</u> from another.' 20 words

Branding on products matters as it gives consumers information and helps distinguish one from another.' (16 words)

News Release #3

MULTI TOUCH DIGITAL INC. HAS ENTERED INTO THE INTERACTIVE TOUCH TABLE INDUSTRY

In addition to many fundamental writing errors, this release ignores the news—that it's introducing a new system, not that the company is entering a new industry. That's important but not as the first information the reader encounters.

Original

Multi Touch Digital Inc. <u>announced today</u> that it has <u>entered into the interactive touch table industry</u> with the release <u>of the Touch Center</u>™, their first product aimed at the consumer market. The Touch Center belongs to a new genre of home entertainment <u>of "tech furniture"</u>. It is an interactive touch computer system embedded in an attractive coffee table design, allowing <u>up to 4 users</u> to learn, work or play either together or independently, using innovative touch technology. "<u>We are pleased to announce</u> that we have successfully entered this market with an important partner, a major Canadian big box retailer," said <u>Bruce Seeley, President and CEO of Multi Touch Digital Inc</u>. 110 words

Edit

Multi Touch Digital Inc. today released the Touch Centre™, its first product aimed at the consumer market, entering the company into the interactive touch table industry. Part of "tech furniture," a new home entertainment genre, Touch Centre, an interactive touch computer system, is embedded in an attractive coffee table design. Up to four users can learn, work or play either together or independently, using innovative touch technology. "We have successfully entered this market with an important partner, a major Canadian big box retailer," said Bruce Seeley, Multi Touch Digital Inc. President and CEO. "This will provide immediate widespread distribution for the product." 93 words, without new quote added; 102 words in all.

Commentary

1. *Announced today* – by issuing a release an announcement is implied; not necessary to say it.

2. *Entered into the interactive touch table industry* – the news here is the system's release, whether or not it joins a new industry

3. *The Touch Center*™ – oddly enough, the company's own website uses Canadian spelling – Centre – to describe the product (https://multitouchdigital.com/multi-touch-coffee-tables). Why American spelling in a Canadian news release?

4. *Their first product* – the company is an 'it.' Their would either be a plural or reference to people.

5. *Part of "tech furniture,"* – Apart from the incorrect publication style quotation format, ", instead of ," placing tech furniture first in the sentence brings up the most important marketing message.

6. *Allowing up to 4 users* – Numbers under 10 are spelled out. Splitting up the sentence also separates the 'embedding' how it will be used.

7. *"We are pleased to announce"* – This remains the biggest cliché in PR writing, as to release anything, one better be estatic about new releases and partnerships. Starting with "We have successfully entered" brings out this thought.

8. *President and CEO of Multi Touch Digital* – Shorter and better as "Bruce Seeley, Multi Touch Digital Inc. President and CEO."

9. *"This will provide"* – I added this quote to balance out the first part and explain why Multi-Touch is so pleased.

News Release #4

2017 YEAR OF SYNCHRONICITY IN GLOBAL GROWTH: SCOTIABANK ECONOMICS GLOBAL OUTLOOK

It's wrong to bury the news, especially when a phrase like 'for the first time' appears. While economics is 'the dismal science,' according to Thomas Carlyle, writing about it need not be. Take a look at these revisions and the reasons for them. The headline and lead can be shortened and be more newsworthy with some simple changes.

Original headline

- 2017 Year of Synchronicity in Global Growth: Scotiabank Economics Global Outlook (11 words and a repeat)
- Synchronicity in 2017: Scotiabank Economics Global Growth Outlook (8 words)

Original lead

Global growth is strengthening as policy stimulus in some advanced economies is unwound. This is a confirmation of the narrative building throughout the year, in which the sources of growth have been broadening across and within countries. (37 words)

"For the first time since the Global Financial Crisis (GFC), all 45 industrialised OECD countries are set to expand," said Jean-François Perrault, Senior Vice President and Chief Economist at Scotiabank. "Given the breadth of growth geographically and its increasing diversity within countries, the foundation remains for solid global performance through at least 2018, though geopolitical risks continue to dominate." (59 words)

Edit

Global growth, strengthening as policy stimulus in some advanced economies unwinds, confirms the narrative building throughout the year: all 45 industrialized OECD countries are expanding for the first time since the Global Financial Crisis (GFC). (35 words, with the news)

"Sources of growth have been broadening across and within countries," said Jean-François Perrault, Scotiabank Senior Vice President and Chief Economist. "Given the breadth of growth geographically and its increasing diversity within countries, the foundation remains for solid global performance through at least 2018, though geopolitical risks continue to dominate." (49 words)

Commentary

- Is strengthening... is unwound – Two uses of "is": it's almost a mortal sin in our lexicon, crying out for editing. See how commas help: 'Global growth, strengthening as policy stimulus in some advanced economies unwinds...' "Strengthening" and "unwinds" are much stronger.
- In which – This sets off an editing alarm; it's awkward in a lead that should be punchy. Note how the real news 'For the first time' is buried in a quote. Move the quote information up to the lead and there is much more of a news story. "All 45 industrialized OECD countries are expanding for the first time since the Global Financial Crisis (GFC)."
- <u>All 45 industrialised – Contemporary style prefers "z."</u> <u>Analyzed, industrialized.</u>
- Senior Vice President and Chief Economist at Scotiabank – Move the bank to the front: Scotiabank SVP and Chief Economist. Even saving one word counts.

News Release #5

'SUMMER CERTIFIED' CANS EXCLUSIVE TO CANADIAN MARKET, SIX LIMITED EDITION DESIGNS COME TO LIFE WHEN EXPOSED TO SUNLIGHT

If the headline was the only part an editor looked at, the product's brand identity would be a mystery in this story. Perhaps it was an effort to emphasize the technology and not over commercialize the product. Even so, including Coors Light in the headline would attract readers more quickly than this mysterious introduction. The headline as it is can be shortened.

A. *'Summer Certified' cans exclusive to Canadian market*
B. *'Summer Certified' cans exclusive to Canada*

However, 'only available in Canada' would be better, as meaning of exclusive is unclear.

Placing the reference to cans first is ineffective. The real news is how they come to life. A better headline would be:

SIX LIMITED 'SUMMER CERTIFIED' COORS LIGHT CAN DESIGNS COME TO LIFE WHEN EXPOSED TO SUNLIGHT
Innovative technology only available in Canada (subhead)

Here is the lead in full:

Original

Coors Light has introduced the world's first beer cans with <u>sun-activated ink technology exclusively to the Canadian market</u>. Available nationwide, the Coors Light Summer Certified cans have six limited edition designs painted in photochromic ink that are <u>nearly invisible until the cans are exposed to UV rays</u>. The moment the cans are brought into sunlight, <u>the vibrant colours of the designs are instantaneously revealed</u>. Coors Light's use of this packaging innovation is a world first in the beverage industry. (80 words)

Edit

Coors Light has introduced Summer Certified, the world's first beer with sun-activated photochromic ink that's nearly invisible until cans are exposed to UV rays in sunlight, instantaneously revealing the design's vibrant colours. Only available in Canada and a beverage industry first, there are six limited edition designs. (47 words).

Commentary

1. *Sun-activated ink technology* – turns into: 'the world's first beer with sun-activated photochromic ink that's nearly invisible until cans are exposed to UV rays in sunlight.' Sun-activated ink technology might be what it is but it doesn't tell the story. Better to specify.

2. *Exclusively to the Canadian market* – Moved to the second sentence, as it wastes precious real estate in the lead. The consumers don't really care if the U.S. or elsewhere has it too, if it's cool enough, as this seems to be.

3. *Nearly invisible.... the vibrant colours of the designs are instantaneously revealed* -- Instantaneously revealing the design's vibrant colours. Use the positive and don't repeat the idea. The most important point is 'instantaneously revealed;' clearly, if they are revealed then they were invisible.

A pause for good writing...sometimes it does work well

CHRIS HODGSON TO PRESENT AT NATIONAL BANK FINANCIAL CONFERENCE

Chris Hodgson, Executive Vice President and Head of Domestic Personal Banking, Scotiabank, will present at National Bank Financial's Canadian Financial Services Conference in Montreal on Wednesday, March 26.

Commentary

It's the way it's supposed to be. Nothing creative but who/what/where/when/why and how, the journalistic basics, executed correctly.

Here is another outstanding news release:

Subaru Canada: Best December Ever, 12 Record Months Lead to Banner Sales and Sixth Consecutive Annual Sales Record

Love the headline-ese! Subaru Canada: Best December Ever. Demonstrates understanding of get-to-the-point headline, with a verb.

Subaru Canada, Inc. (SCI) rings in a new year delightfully announcing an unprecedented sales streak with 12 consecutive months of ever-increasing results. This past month capped a record-breaking year with 3,876 units retailed, a 4.6 percent increase over the same month last year and best December ever. More importantly, these milestone results culminate in a banner sales year with a grand total of 54,570 vehicles retailed in 2017. This annual sales record surpasses last year's record of 50,190 units, for a record-breaking 8.7 percent increase in overall sales.

Many releases of course make the fundamental error of saying 'we are pleased to announce' but in this, Subaru is proud of something but characterizes the announcement 'delightfully,' a great touch, rather than the company's itself being proud, which of course it is. It's an excellent move, as is simply the tenor of the entire release, which actually has news to report.

News Release #6

Canadian Canines Crowned for Saving Lives: From 92 to 64 words

Nice try with alliteration.

Try this:

A. Canadian canines crowned for saving lives
B. Canadian lifesaving canines crowned

The alliteration still works. Another possibility...

Three heroic hounds welcomed into this year's Purina Animal Hall of Fame

Again, the alliteration is at work but in the dog universe, hounds are a specific animal group, including Afghan, Basset and Blood hounds, Beagles, Borzois, etc., and to dog lovers (the awards' audience) the word hound even though it is not capitalized can be misleading. http://www.ckc.ca/en/Choosing-a-Dog/Choosing-a-Breed/Hounds

Better headline:
Three heroes welcomed into Purina Animal Hall of Fame
It's simpler and shorter and doesn't confuse the dog fan

Original lead

Pets have long been considered our most trusted companions and it's easy to see why. They make our lives feel bigger, better and frequently seem to understand us more than we understand ourselves. This unique intuitive connection between humans and pets is often best exemplified by the heroic animal stories that continue to amaze the world. Today, Purina is thrilled to announce three new canine heroes who have been inducted into the Purina Animal Hall of Fame, each of whom has a remarkable tale about the day they saved their owners' lives. (92 words)

Edit

Pets, long been considered our most trusted companions, make our lives feel happier and better. They frequently understand us better than we understand ourselves. Heroic animal stories exemplify the unique intuitive connection between humans and pets, continually amazing the world. Today, Purina inducted three new canine heroes into the Purina Animal Hall of Fame, each having a remarkable tale about saving their owner's life. (64 words)

Commentary

1. *'Easy to see why'* – If that's so, then show it don't say it.
2. *'Seem to understand us'* – Seem just weakens it; either they do or don't.
3. *'By the heroic animal stories'* -- Passive voice alarm bell rang loudly here.
4. *'Continue to amaze'* -- Continue is almost always unnecessary. Continually amazing the world is shorter and better.

5. *'Thrilled to announce'* -- For shame, number one error in news releases—of course you are thrilled, that's why there's a news release. Wholly unnecessary.

6. *'Each of whom'* -- Each is sufficient; of whom adds nothing.

News Release #7

10 ways to reduce 25 per cent from a release

In this release, by applying a few basic Better Writing tips, a 25 per cent reduction is easily achieved – with the same meaning. Repeating 'in which' twice, an insult to the language, is also deleted.

Original

Even with new investments in affordability, Ontario remains most expensive province in which to pursue higher education (17 words)

Ontario remains the most expensive province in which to pursue post-secondary education, according to data released today by Statistics Canada. Average undergraduate tuition fees for the 2017-2018 academic year will be $8,454, up from $8,114 in the previous year. Across the country, graduate and international tuition fees also continued to rise, signaling an alarming reliance by post-secondary institutions on tuition fees as a primary source of revenue. **(67 words)**

Edits

Even with enhanced affordability, Ontario higher education tuition most expensive in Canada (12 words)

Ontario's post-secondary tuition remains Canada's most expensive, according to Statistics Canada data released today. For the 2017-2018 academic year, average undergraduate tuition fees are $8,454, up from $8,114 in 2016. Graduate and international tuition fees also rose nationally, signaling post-secondary institutions' alarming reliance on them as a primary revenue source. (50 words)

Commentary

1. *New investments in affordability* – this isn't followed up in the lead and isn't clear. It can be shortened to 'enhanced affordability.'
2. *In which* – one of those phrases that should send writers scurrying for the editing pen. It's repeated in both the headline and the lead, is awkward both times – and easily eliminated.
3. *Headline writing* – Headline-ese is a special craft and suspends normal grammatical rules. In the rewrite, the verb isn't used or needed.
4. *According to data released by Statistics Canada* – avoid the passive voice, avoid the passive voice! Make it: 'according to Statistics Canada data released today.' Later transpose so it's 'post-secondary institutions' alarming reliance.' Use the glorious apostrophe; it's a passive voice killer. See the 'Of' chapter.
5. *Will be* – we are already in the 2017 academic year, so just 'are.'
6. *In the previous year* – 2016 covers it.
7. *Across the country* – 'nationally' reduces three words to one and can be placed later in the sentence.
8. *Continued to rise* – another construction to be avoided. 'Also rose' has the same meaning.

Word repeats – a simple tip: if you use the same phrase twice, cut the second one. 'On them' easily refers to the earlier 'tuition fees.'

Primary revenue source of revenue – Of is and by has helped this flabby lead and here 'source of revenue' becomes 'revenue source.'

News Release #8

Five ways to make a lead clearer and reduce 137 words to 99, nearly 28 per cent

It would be easy to say: what are they smoking? In addition to word reductions, with this story about a pot producer, there are many extra words, redundancies and passive voices. Look how it can be cleaned up.

Original headline and edit

Growth Corporation is ~~proud to introduce~~ *Spectrum Cannabis* to the Canadian medical cannabis market.

Growth Corporation introduces *Spectrum Cannabis* to Canadian medical cannabis market.

Original lead

The new Canadian brand identity, already <u>launched in several jurisdictions around the world</u>, is a progression of the Mettrum Spectrum and is inspired by the industry-first strain classification system which <u>simplifies the dialogue around strength and dosage</u> by categorizing medical cannabis according to THC and CBD levels, using a straightforward colour-coded guide. (52 words)

In place since 2014 under the Mettrum brand, the Spectrum has been <u>well received by</u> the medical community and <u>equally adopted by customers</u> who regularly shop by Spectrum. The rebranding of Mettrum Health to Spectrum Cannabis in Canada is the natural progression <u>of this methodology</u> and will ensure a consistent and recognizable global brand across all <u>federally legal jurisdictions</u> where Canopy Growth operates. (137 words)

Edit

Canopy Growth Corporation has introduced *Spectrum Cannabis*, the industry-first colour-coded strain classification system, to the Canadian medical cannabis market.

Already launched in several international jurisdictions, *Spectrum Cannabis*, building on the Mettrum Spectrum, simplifies the dialogue around strength and dosage, categorizing medical cannabis according to THC and CBD levels.

The medical community and regular Spectrum customers have both adopted the system, in place in Canada since 2014 under the Mettrum brand. With Mettrum's rebranding as *Spectrum Cannabis*, this methodology's natural progression will ensure consistency and awareness in all jurisdictions where Canopy Growth operates. (99 words)

Commentary

1. *Proud to introduce Spectrum Cannabis to the Canadian medical cannabis market* – Apart from making the #1 PR mistake, 'proud to introduce,' which is obvious since a news release is being issued, this is a missed opportunity to explain Spectrum Cannabis. Better to say:
2. *Canopy Growth Corporation has introduced Spectrum Cannabis, the industry-first colour-coded strain classification system, to the Canadian medical cannabis market.*
3. *Launched in several jurisdictions around the world* – 'Around the world' can usually be said in one word, global or international. Here 'international' is clearer and more accurate; it's not apparently global yet. In addition, the

sentence itself is 52 words, too lengthy for a news release. Break it up:

4. Already launched in several international jurisdictions, Spectrum Cannabis, building on the Mettrum Spectrum, simplifies the dialogue around strength and dosage, categorizing medical cannabis according to THC and CBD levels.

5. Well received by... equally adopted by... shop by Spectrum – Three passive voices in one sentence! I can hear Of Is and By adherents choking on this. Try this:
   - The medical community and regular Spectrum customers have both adopted the system, in place in Canada since 2014 under the Mettrum brand.

6. The rebranding of Mettrum Health... of this methodology – Don't forget to eliminate 'of' where possible. "With Mettrum Health's rebranding" and 'this methodology's natural progression.'

7. *Will ensure a consistent and recognizable global brand across all federally legal jurisdictions* – Works better as: 'consistency and awareness in all jurisdictions where Canopy Growth operates.' 'Federally legal' is redundant. The company wouldn't be operating it if were not legal, anywhere and not all jurisdictions would be federal – jurisdictions is description enough.

News Release #9

It's not just reducing the lead from 104 to 85 words, it's understanding what's news!

For some reason, the cannabis industry might not be holding up good writing standards; hope it's not for the reasons we might think. Now comes Legalize Private Retail and the comments cover understanding what's news, while also reducing the word count. The group commissioning a study is not news. When it occurred isn't either, nor is why it was done. The headline is also a mess.

Original headline

Most Albertans Favour Private Cannabis Retail <u>According to Legalize Private Retail's Public Opinion Research</u>

According to Legalize Private Retail's Public Opinion Research – Just not necessary to say who did the study; a subhead would be better. Try simply:

Most Albertans (59 per cent) Favour Private Cannabis Retail, Study Finds

Original lead

<u>Legalize Private Retail commissioned a public opinion research survey between</u> November 10 and 15, 2017, <u>to determine the level of support</u> for private cannabis retail in Alberta. Key findings show that a majority of Albertans support private cannabis retail, confirming that the <u>Government of Alberta</u> made the right decision in adopting a <u>private retail</u> model for Alberta.

The research shows that initial support for <u>private cannabis retail</u> is <u>46%</u>, but when Albertans are made aware of the level of government regulation and oversight that will exist in a private system, and the cost-savings from government not owning and operating stores, support increases to 59%. (104 words)

Edit

A majority of Albertans (59 per cent) support keeping cannabis sales in private hands, according to Legalize Private Retail's just released research. The results confirm and support Alberta's decision to adopt private retail when recreational cannabis becomes legally available. The Legalize group stated its study showed that initial support for private sales was 46 per cent, which rose to 59 per cent when respondents understood the cost-savings from government not owning and operating stores as well as regulatory oversight existing in a private system. (84 words, 20 per cent reduction).

Commentary

1. *Legalize Private Retail commissioned a public opinion research survey* – No two ways about it; everyone commissions a survey. It just isn't news.

2. *To determine the level of support* – A basic rule would be not to say why you did it in the lead; that can be explained much later. (The news is: the results. Get to them right away.

3. *Government of Alberta* – An Of Is and By pet peeve: the government would call itself that but what is Alberta but a government, so leave it just as 'Alberta.' It saves two words.

4. *A private retail/ private cannabis retail* – With the name of the organization Legalize Private Retail, there has to be other ways of not repeating this over and over. Try synonyms. They work.

5. *Support increases to 59%* – This is the very latest point in the original lead. It's the news. Note how the revision moves it up to the first sentence and the headline. And CP Style is 59 per cent not 59 %.

News Release #10

Six ways to reduce a lead 17.3 per cent—from 75 to 62 words.
This release is decently well written and quite understandable, though it makes basic mistakes and can be more concise

Original

Lionsgate today announced the launch of the educational initiative THE WONDER CERTIFIED KIND CLASSROOM. The program is inspired by R.J. Palacio's worldwide bestselling children's novel and Lionsgate's upcoming film Wonder, starring Academy Award® winner Julia Roberts, Jacob Tremblay and Owen Wilson, slated for release on November 17th. *Wonder* tells the heartwarming story of Auggie Pullman, a boy born with facial differences who can't blend in because he was born to stand out. (75 words)

Edit

Lionsgate today launched THE WONDER CERTIFIED KIND CLASSROOM educational initiative, inspired by R.J. Palacio's bestselling children's novel, and Lionsgate's upcoming film *Wonder*, starring Academy Award® winner Julia Roberts, Jacob Tremblay and Owen Wilson. Slated for release on November 17, Wonder tells Auggie Pullman's heartwarming story; due to facial differences, he can't blend in. He was born to stand out. (62 words)

Commentary

1. *Today announced* – The release covers the announcement; no need to mention it. 'Today launched' is much more direct.

2. *Of the educational initiative* – Of course, get rid of 'of,' the basic lesson. 'The classroom educational initiative' is shorter and better.

3. *Is inspired by* – Normally, I'd say get rid of 'by,' too. But making it the novel inspired it, more active, doesn't work. Sometimes the passive voice must stand.

4. *Academy Award*® – No editor ever uses the ® mark but in the case of the Oscars® (which would be a shorter and identical use), the Motion Picture Academy rigorously enforces its trademark, so be careful.

5. *Slated for release/Nov. 17th* – Style mistake; it's Nov. 17. Better to put in the period in after Owen Wilson. When in doubt add a period; it makes most sentences better. Had some desire to add IDs for Tremblay "Room" and Wilson but didn't change it.

6. *Story of Auggie Pullman* – Easy to get rid of the 'of.' 'Auggie Pullman's story,' but the following part is confusing. It would have been sufficient to say 'due to facial differences, he can't blend in. Using the period, gives it an emphatic last sentence. 'He was born to stand out.' Use periods. They really help.

News Release #11

Reducing a lead by nearly 24 words or 21 per cent, and switching paragraphs one and two for clarity

In this news release, the first two paragraphs should be reversed to avoid burying the news. Talking about 'drug-impaired' driving on the rise is well and good but it isn't what the news story is about. If it were, then it would be justified as the lead but the news comes in the second paragraph—launching a public awareness campaign. This is also reflected in the headline, which is about the campaign. The best news stories proceed from the headline to the lead amplifying the same information. The lead explains the headline. In this one, the headline correctly assesses the news, then it reverts to the background. The revision, different from the other examples, will be followed by the original, with commentary.

The edit is first, as that's the way to understand the mistakes in the original

Don't drive high: public awareness campaign launches today

Hon. Ralph Goodale, Minister of Public Safety and Emergency Preparedness, launched a new public awareness campaign communicating the risk associated with driving under the influence of cannabis and other drugs. Canadians will soon see ads in public spaces, on social media, on television and in movie theatres with evidence-based information about hazardous drug-impaired driving. (54 words)

Since Canadian police-reported data became available in 2009, drug-impaired driving has been clearly rising and significantly contributes to fatal road crashes. Young people, the largest group dying in vehicle crashes, also most often test positive for drugs. 37 words (91 words in total)

Original

Drug-impaired driving has been on the rise in Canada since police-reported data became available in 2009 <u>and is a major</u> contributor to fatal road crashes in Canada. <u>Young people continue to be the</u> largest group of drivers who die in crashes and test positive for drugs. (46 words)

Today, the Honourable Ralph Goodale, Minister of Public Safety and Emergency Preparedness, launched the Government of Canada's drug-impaired driving public awareness campaign to communicate to Canadians the risks associated with driving under the influence of cannabis and other drugs. Canadians will soon see ads in public spaces, on social media, on television and in movie theatres. Public awareness efforts will include evidence-based information on the risks of drug-impaired driving. 69 words (115 words in total)

Commentary

1. *Hon. Ralph Goodale* – Even 'Hon.' isn't strictly necessary except to plump up the minister. 'The Honourable' is overkill.
2. *Government of Canada's* – Canada is sufficient and shorter.
3. *Drug-impaired driving public awareness campaign to communicate to Canadians* – launched a new public awareness campaign communicating the risk associated with driving under the influence of cannabis and other drugs.
   - The revision moves the campaign's rationale closer to the news, and in a news release from Ottawa from a minister hardly needs to explain that it's communicating to Canadians.
4. *Young people continue to be the* largest group of drivers who die in crashes and test positive for drugs. Or: Young people, the largest group dying in vehicle crashes, also most often test positive for drugs. Use those comma clauses and get rid of 'continue' wherever possible.

News Release #12

Too much time to get to the news

It's bad enough that video peers into Texas schools but this dreadful news release wastes money, as it takes so much time to get to the news. No one but no one, particularly an overworked editor, will ever read through the 57 words of stultifying company explanations before the announcement.

In the edit, company descriptions are shortened greatly, with word repetitions (a leading provider/ the leading global provider) eliminated. Then the actual news is reduced from 27 words to 21. The lead is then reduced from 79 words to 62, a nearly 22 per cent reduction.

Original

Hikvision USA, Inc., <u>a leading provider of artificial intelligence,</u> <u>machine learning,</u> <u>robotics and other emerging technologies,</u> <u>and the world's largest manufacturer</u> of video surveillance products and solutions, and Eagle Eye Networks, <u>the leading</u> <u>global provider of cloud-based video surveillance solutions</u> <u>addressing the needs of</u> businesses, schools, alarm companies, security integrators, and individuals, today announced a video surveillance solution that enables Texas school districts to immediately comply with the video surveillance requirements set forth in Texas Senate Bill 507 (SB-507). (79 words)

Edit

Hikvision USA, Inc., and Eagle Eye Networks, today announced a video surveillance solution enabling Texas school districts to comply immediately with Texas Senate Bill 507's video surveillance requirements. The world's largest surveillance manufacturer, Hikvision also provides artificial intelligence, machine learning, robotics and other emerging technologies. Eagle Eye's cloud-based video solutions serve businesses, schools, alarm companies, security integrators, and individuals globally. (62 words, nearly 22 per cent reduction)

Commentary

1. *A leading provider/ the leading global provider* – This phrase is often used when a company doesn't want to give itself an industry ranking—largest provider, number three provider. If the organization is indeed the world's largest, then say so as this release does. Otherwise it's only self-applied corporate bumpf.

2. *The world's largest manufacturer of video surveillance products and solutions* -- The world's largest video surveillance manufacturer. Here the 'of' is removed and as it's a throw away clause anyway, it was moved to the sentence's beginning.

3. *The leading global provider of cloud-based video surveillance solutions addressing the needs of* -- Using the possessive here gets rid of several words (Eagle Eye's) and 'addressing the needs of' becomes simply serves; the meaning is the same.

4. **That enables Texas school districts to immediately comply with the video surveillance requirements set forth in Texas Senate Bill 507 (SB-507)** – Avoiding split infinitives 'to immediately comply' has gone out of style but here 'to comply immediately' is stronger. A possessive again comes to the rescue with 'Bill 507's video surveillance requirements.' That eliminates 'set forth' and the strange repeat of Bill 507 and the Bill number.

News Release #13

Puzzling news release of the day.

Here is what I mean when I am astonished that professionals disburse funds to release something like this, which buries the news; uses passive voices, does not make a dull topic interesting, which is what it should. Here is how applying Better Writer tips turns it around.

Original

While most read parts of privacy policies, many admit they do not read them at all

In a study commissioned and guided by the Canadian Marketing Association (CMA)'s Privacy and Data Advisory Committee, it was found that consumers want to read privacy policies, but they have to be user-friendly.

Edit

Most Canadians don't read privacy policies, many read only parts, study says

Consumers would read user-friendly privacy policies but find privacy policies them too long and difficult to understand, according to a new Canadian Marketing Association (CMA)'s Privacy and Data Advisory Committee study. One quarter admit they don't read policies at all, the study said.

Commentary

Headline

Many admit they do not read them at all—this is really the news; it's obvious that most would not. They're boring and who cares?

Lead

1. *In a study commissioned and guided by* – starting with a passive voice is a no-no. Not sure of the difference between 'commissioned' and 'guided by.' If you commission it, you are guiding it.

2. *It was found that consumers want to read privacy policies* – this is also a passive. Two in one lead; not quite a record but almost.

3. *The news doesn't come until deep in the second paragraph*: "It identified that while most Canadians say they read parts of privacy policies, one quarter admit they don't read policies at all..." Also 'It identified that' can be eliminated as can most other 'it' clauses...it seems that, I think that.

News Release #14

The sin of dullness and missing detail

This news release, not that badly written, commits the sin of dullness, and missing detail. Of Is and By didn't reduce many words, just made it more interesting. News sense means everything.

Original

Mattamy Homes, North America's largest privately owned homebuilder, will <u>host a lively grand-opening event</u> on Saturday, March 10, to showcase Stillwater, the company's first master-planned community <u>in the City of Edmonton</u>.

Additional detail in release's last paragraph:

'To tour the new sales centre and seven fully decorated model homes, as well as enjoy food trucks and family entertainment.

Embraces the nature around it, mixing parks, trails and green space. The highlight is a naturalized wetland area that is strategically paired with a storm pond.'

Edit

Mattamy Homes, North America's largest privately owned homebuilder, will host a lively grand-opening event on Saturday, March 10, including food trucks and family entertainment, to showcase Stillwater, its first Edmonton master-planned community. With a highlighted naturalized wetland area, strategically paired with a storm pond, Stillwater embraces surrounding nature, mixing parks, trails and green space.

Commentary

1. *A lively grand opening event* – It doesn't say much and doesn't attract the reader. What is lively? Why should we attend? Note how the detail from the last paragraph makes it more interesting: 'including food trucks and family entertainment.'
2. *Community in the City of Edmonton* – an essential Of Is and By rule is 'eliminate unnecessary geographical designations, like 'City of.' Edmonton, unmistakably a city, can be moved

in front of 'master-planned,' with 'company' eliminated. Better as: 'its first Edmonton master-planned community.'

News Release #15

91 to 72 words, a 20 per cent reduction, and shorter headlines too

Open Table, a service I often use, provides much-needed dining out efficiency. Applying this writing system to its news release achieves the same meaning with fewer words, making it easier and shorter to read. In this Open Table example, with a 91 to 72 word reduction, many extraneous words fall away easily.

Original

Toronto and Montreal Claim Highest Number of Restaurants with Bustling Bar Scenes, Entertainment and Ambience (15 words)

It's been a long winter. Now that spring is here, Canadians are preparing to pack away the winter boots and step back into the nightlife. To guide them to the latest buzzing spots for a night out, OpenTable, the world's leading provider of online restaurant reservations and part of Bookings Holdings, Inc. (NASDAQ: BKNG), has announced the 100 Best Restaurants in Canada for a Big Night Out. These awards reflect the combined opinions of more than 550,000 restaurant reviews submitted by verified OpenTable diners for more than 2,500 restaurants in Canada. (91 words)

Edit

Toronto and Montreal: most restaurants with bustling bar scenes, entertainment and ambience (12 words)

It's been a long winter. Now that spring is here, Canadians are packing away winter boots and stepping out. For a guide to the latest buzzy night spots, <u>OpenTable</u>, the world's leading online restaurant reservations provider, part of <u>Bookings Holdings, Inc.</u> (NASDAQ: <u>BKNG</u>), has announced the 100 Best Canadian Restaurants for a Big Night Out. The awards reflect verified OpenTable diners' combined opinions from more than 550,000 reviews covering 2,500 Canada restaurants. (72 words)

Here are the A and B comparisons, demonstrating the key edits.

A. Canadians are preparing to pack away the winter boots
B. Canadians are packing away winter boots

Putting away boots is pretty simple, doesn't require much preparation. Using 'the' is unnecessary too.

A. And step back into the nightlife
B. Stepping out

Spring does encourage more going out but it's not only nightlife, which is misleading, too, with its sense of nightclubs and bars. Restaurants operate at other times; stepping out keeps the idea generic covering day and night.

A. To guide them to the latest buzzing spots for a night out
B. For a guide to the latest buzzy night spots

'Them' is not necessary and the spots themselves don't buzz; they are buzzy. 'The latest buzzy night spots' accomplishes much more in fewer words.

A. The world's leading provider of online restaurant reservations
B. The world's leading online restaurant reservations provider

'Of' is easily eliminated.

A. Has announced the 100 Best Restaurants <u>in Canada</u> for a Big Night Out-

B. Has announced the 100 Best <u>Canadian</u> Restaurants for a Big Night Out

Watch the word 'in,' as it's a sign of something that can turn into a modifier...in Canada/Canadian.

A. These awards reflect the combined opinions of more than 550,000 restaurant reviews submitted by verified OpenTable diners for more than 2,500 restaurants in Canada. (25 words)

B. The awards reflect verified OpenTable diners' combined opinions from more than 550,000 reviews covering 2,500 Canadian restaurants. (18 words)

Reducing from 25 to 18 words (or 28 per cent) helps but more importantly the superfluous words 'of, submitted, by, for and in' are all how the Better Writer system can help most copy.

News Release #15 and additional copy

Part 1

Editing Tangerine's company promises, reducing headlines from 11 to 6 words, and a lead from 86 to 62 words

In a recent LinkedIn jobs post, Tangerine, the innovative on-line banker, was seeking an internal writer/editor so I wondered what the company's writing might be like (and thought I could help). Here's what I found: Tangerine definitely needs an editor. For a highly progressive company, more attention needs to be paid to writing basics.

Original headline and lead

Canadians Facing Barriers When It Comes to Investing for First Time (11 words)

Lack of money, risk tolerance, and knowledge preventing Canadians from investing their money

<u>A recent survey* by Tangerine Investments</u> found that over a third of Canadians surveyed (36 percent) <u>do not have an investment account</u>, and only four percent of non-investors have ever seriously considered opening one. <u>When asked to select the</u> reasons why they don't invest, 70 percent of non-investors <u>said they don't have enough money</u>, 25 percent said they're worried about the risk of losing money, and 20 percent said they don't know enough about investing their money, and it's too complex. (86 words)

Part 2

First Time Canadian Investors Face Barriers (6 words)

Lack of money, risk tolerance, and knowledge hinder investors

Tangerine Investments' recent survey found that over a third of Canadians (36 percent) are without an investment account, and only four percent seriously consider opening one. Reasons for not investing include scarce funds (70 percent) and fear of financial loss (25 percent), while 20 percent said investing is too complex and they don't know enough about it. (62 words)

Commentary

A. Note the changes from A to B; the meaning is the same but the word count is not.
B. A recent survey by Tangerine Investments

C. Tangerine Investments' recent survey

D. Do not have an investment account

E. Are without an investment account

F. When asked to select reasons why they don't invest

G. Reasons for not investing

H. Said they don't have enough money

I. Scarce funds

We Dare means challenging the status quo, and innovating on behalf of our Clients - providing them with the best possible experience. (22 words)

A. We Dare – challenging the status quo and innovating and providing Clients - with the best possible experience. (18 words)

The – connects the two thoughts and renders the redundant word 'mean' unnecessary. 'On behalf of clienst' becomes 'providing for clients.'

A. We Care means we work tirelessly for our Clients and value the needs and uniqueness of all of our colleagues at Tangerine. (22 words)

B. We Care means working tirelessly for Clients and valuing our Tangerine colleagues' needs and uniqueness. (15 words)

'We work tirelessly' is better and shorter as 'working tirelessly.' 'Of all of our colleagues at Tangerine has 'of' twice, an Of Is and By no-no, and the 'at' clause triggers moving Tangerine in front of 'colleagues.'

Here are a few more A and B examples.

A. We Share reflects the desire to make a difference which is at the heart of our culture. It's empowering our Clients with the knowledge and tools to take charge of their financial future. (33 words)

B. We Share, the heart of our culture, means making a difference, empowering our Clients with the knowledge and tools to direct their financial future. (24 words)

C. We Deliver is the power of keeping our Promises. It's how we redefine our Clients' banking experiences in ways they never imagined possible (23 words)

D. We Deliver, the power of keeping Promises, redefines Clients' banking experiences in ways never imagined possible. (16 words)

Finally, even the ad itself can be shortened:

A. Reporting to the Manager, Writing Services, the Writer & Proofreader is responsible for writing, editing and proofreading marketing materials to ensure they meet the needs of internal stakeholders and adhere to internal guidelines. (33 words)

B. Reporting to the Manager, Writing Services, the Writer & Proofreader writes, edits and proofreads marketing materials, ensuring they meet internal stakeholders needs and adhere to internal guidelines. (27 words)

Section IV:
Putting It All Together
With Exercises

Try to edit the examples...

Chapter 21

1. Of and In

Original

<u>In celebration of the</u> new North Expansion, CF Sherway Gardens will be hosting on Monday September 21, an exclusive fashion show and cocktail party.

Edit

<u>To celebrate the new</u> North Expansion, CF Sherway Gardens will host an exclusive fashion show and cocktail party Monday Sept. 21.

Commentary

It's not just 'of' here that can be eliminated; to celebrate is cleaner than 'in celebration of.' In addition, note that the fashion show is moved before the date. By doing that, the 'on' is removed. What it is, the show, is more important than the date, the when.

2. Singular or plural?

Original

Media who attends The Front Row <u>have the opportunity to speak with</u> the show's <u>producer</u>, Hans Koechling

Edit

Media attending THE FRONT ROW can speak with the show's producer, Hans Koechling.

Commentary

Media is both a collective noun—the media is expected to show up—and the Latin plural of medium. Despite significant debate favouring media being always plural—the media are expected to show up—contemporary usage weighs in on the side of it being both singular and plural, as in 'Cinema and video are two different media.' However, the edit here—changing 'media who attends' shows how media can be misunderstood as it should be 'media who attend,' in the singular. Using the gerund 'media attending' eliminates the confusion.

3. <u>Correct style for titles?</u>

As a basic idea, put titles before the name and only capitalize political or military but not occupational titles.

Original

Wayne Barwise, Executive Vice President for Cadillac Fairview

Edit

Cadillac Fairview executive vice president Wayne Barwise

Commentary

Prime Minister Justin Trudeau

French President Emmanuel Macron

General George Marshall

4. <u>Who does it refer to? Is Of and dollar signs</u>

In this example, apart from the edits, the young man in question appears to be the offspring of the company not the family.

Original

Marco Muzzo is the grandson of Marel Contractors, worth <u>1.7 billion</u> dollars and ranked as the 52nd wealthiest Canadian family and he faces numerous charges.

Edit

Marco Muzzo, grandson of Marel Contractors' founder, ranked as the 52nd wealthiest Canadian, worth $1.7 billion, faces numerous charges.

Commentary

In the quest to eliminate 'of,' it could be 'Marel Contractors' founder's grandson' but it's a mouthful and demonstrates how good judgement sometimes prevents following these tips too slavishly. But we do change 'Marco Muzzo is the grandson' to Marco Muzzo, grandson of…' and then reverse the rank and the amount. Never spell out dollars when a dollar sign is used; it means dollars and $1.7 billion is correct.

5. <u>It or They</u>?

A splendid example of the 'it' and 'they' suggestions in action, the next sentence shows how easy it is to confuse them.

Original

The Muzzo family has offered <u>their</u> sympathies to the Naville-Lake family <u>on account of</u> their son's actions.

Edit

The Muzzo family has offered <u>its</u> sympathies to the Naville-Lake family due to their son's actions.

Commentary

Although families comprise people, they are still an organizational unit, so refer to them as an 'it,' while as a plural referring to the son is a 'their.' 'Due to' is shorter and better than 'on account of.'

Shorten titles and use the 'of' tips

A. Heather McGregor, <u>CEO of the YWCA</u>, will comment on the significance and impact <u>of those</u> contributions.

B. YWCA CEO Heather McGregor, will comment on the contributions' significance and impact.

Always put titles first; move contributions with a possessive before 'significance and impact' and eliminating 'of' works its magic charm.

Of and by

A. You are invited to attend the announcement <u>of the competition winners by</u> Mayor Tory.

B. You are invited to attend Mayor Tory's announcement <u>of the competition winners</u>.

C. Mayor Tory invites you to the competition winner's announcement.

Two alternatives for shortening this one.

Word repeats

A. Before the match we invite you to a <u>press conference</u> at 11:45 a.m. The press conference will feature team captain, Christine Sinclair and coach <u>of the</u> team, John Herdman.

B. Before the match join us for a <u>press conference</u> at 11:45 a.m., featuring Canadian captain, Christine Sinclair and team coach John Herdman.

Another instance where a gerund (featuring) can link two formerly separate sentences, and make the information more active. Of course we also got rid of an 'of.'

Is again

A. The city's newest museum is the first dedicated to Boston's modern history, with artifacts and exhibitions showcasing the 1920's to the present.

B. The city's newest museum, the first dedicated to Boston's modern history, showcases artifacts and exhibitions from the 1920s to the present.

Always make the verb active and closer to the subject: 'showcases artifacts.'

Of and is

The upcoming exhibition <u>at the Art Institute</u> called *Anatomically Correct* is a group show <u>of</u> portraiture photography on the hot topic issue <u>of</u> body image. (25 words)

Anatomically Correct, the upcoming <u>Art Institute</u> portraiture photography show, features a hot topic, body image. (15 words)

This revision contains several of the book's lessons all at once. They are:

1. Locations with introductions 'at the Art Institute' can almost always turn into modifiers.

2. Words like 'called' are extra descriptors. Note how moving *Anatomically Correct* to the beginning removes the need for 'called.' Always try and avoid that.

3. 'A group show of...' can be moved to follow Art Institute and made shorter, too.

4. 'The hot topic issue <u>of</u> body image' has an 'of,' a redundancy in 'hot topic issue,' and is simpler as a 'hot topic, body image.'

Another example:

A. The performance will take place on Wednesday, June 17 at 10 a.m. in the Moos Gallery located at 622 Richmond Street West.

B. The performance will take place on Wednesday, June 17 at 10 a.m. in the Moos Gallery, 622 Richmond Street West.

Section V: The 10 best PR Tools
– a career reflection

Chapter 22

In 2019, The PR Writer published a four-part series, outlining all that I knew about the best PR tools. The idea happened to be trending on Google so it was opportune. I am excerpting it here, in the interest of assisting those following PR careers.

Part I

Do a quick Google search for PR Tools and there are many posts devoted to what's available on line that will help distribute and track PR information or locate new PR outlets. It's surprising how much there is to discover about PR activities. Even though discussions of content and how to make it better are minimal.

PR Tools for media relations

Many bloggers will tell you the Top 10 PR tools include finding journalists with Muck Rack, BlogDash and Anewstip. Or that contact details are made easy with Connectifier, Sell Hack and Anymail Finder. Or to distribute and monitor releases, go to Agility, PRWeb, or Canada Newswire, PR Newswire, both Cision properties, Business Wire or Marketwired.

PR Tools for SEO

Those more interested in social media will point to SEMrush for key word research (which I use and can vouch for), Ahrefs **for backlinks,** Moz **an all purpose SEO wizard or** FirstSiteGuide **for web performance analysis.**

There are also many PR tools for writing. But not necessarily for content.

Top PR tools for writing

The most well-known PR Tool for writing is Grammarly. As its website states, "Grammarly is an online grammar and spelling checker that improves communication by helping users find and correct writing mistakes."

The Most Dangerous Writing App is an interesting PR Tool. Before starting, set a session length – minutes or words. Write and don't stop. Hesitate for more than five seconds, and it deletes everything. Complete your session, and it saves your work. The idea is to make you write and not stop.

CoSchedule Headline Analyzer scores your headline and its ability to convert SEO, social shares, or increased traffic. Write a great headline kicks ass, and your outreach message invites clicks.

The Hemingway Editor App offers an extra and impartial pair of eyes to check work. An interactive editing tool, it highlights grammatical errors, excessive passive voice, complex sentences and common mistakes. Word count and a readability scores are there too. Interestingly, Hemingway, the great author, is undergoing some reassessment in light of #metoo. Why do we still read him, the Daily Beast recently asked.

What's needed before using those PR tools

At the same time, while there are writing tools, and work well. But they don't answer the fundamental question: if you get readers there what are you going to say—and how are you going to say it? Not only that, does it fit within generally accepted character counts for titles, tags, headlines and even copy? Too often all those are ignored, with all the flabby writing out there.

Part II

PR Tools: What do PR people do?

Although the PR profession is well established, most people still mostly have little or no idea what do PR people do and what public relations tools they use? They wonder what a typical day is like, and what is the work of PR and what are PR skills. All the negative stereotypes come forward -- spinmeister, flack and today even liar. In addition, where dissembling even at the highest levels of government has become a daily practice, misunderstanding about PR people is at highest level ever. Even Richard Nixon looks like an honest man in the age of Trump.

PR specialists have many activities but its most important is managing reputations, for without positive public acceptance, there will be reluctance to buy products and services from companies with very poor reputations. I hate to keep bringing this up, but the Trump brand is forever sullied due to what has been exposed in Washington about malfeasance, corruption and dishonesty. That's the last time I will mention that name in this story.

How do you become a PR person?

A career in PR demands something important: gaining understanding and support for clients, as well influencing public opinion and behaviour. What does that require? A keen understanding both of clients and the public. What makes them tick is essential; how to act as the bridge between both is the PR person's role. This is the most important answer to the question what do PR people do?

Although PR and marketing can be very similar, their goals significantly vary. PR efforts, boosting or protecting brand reputation, may not always have an impact on sales. PR professionals create contact and often use indirect means, such as promoting brands through press release writing and speaking at industry events, However, marketing campaigns only drive sales – their only purpose. Nothing else. Instead improving public perceptions, marketing focuses on driving revenue and boosting profits – while not damaging reputations.

Understanding media is the key to PR success. That hasn't changed with the advent of social media, which if anything has enhanced the idea of media savvy's overwhelming importance.

Media builds, maintains and manage client reputations. It also manages practitioners' images as we as individuals are as much a brand as are corporations, public entities or services, and charitable organizations.

What PR pros do is communicate are key messages to defined publics establishing – specific influential groups. With the key publics or targets audiences identified, the communicators maintain goodwill and understanding between an organization and the target audiences. Once media is engaged, PR professionals must monitor it constantly. Research discovers the stake holders concerns and expectations and whether the media strategy is working. You'll then report and explain the findings to its management. PR specialists deal with many kinds of media; this is a major distinction between it and advertising. Here are a few types:

Media: Owned vs. Paid vs. Earned

Public relations can be split into three categories: owned, paid, and earned media. Each works towards the same reputation-building goal but use different strategies to get there.

Guess what? Your PR skills should include using all three.

Owned Media

Defined as any content that you control, owned media is often the go-to strategy for businesses looking to <u>build a PR campaign</u>.

And, rightly so: It's arguably the most important type of PR-related media that you should be focusing on because you have total control (unlike the other two tactics).

Owned media can range from:

- Social media posts
- Blog content
- Website copy

It has the aim of acting as a virtual home for your PR activity. People writing about your brand or products are likely to reference owned media in their own coverage.

Paid Media

You likely already know that paying to promote your content is pretty standard in the marketing world. That's no different when it comes to PR.

Paid media refers to paying to make your content visible. It's common practice for PR professionals to promote owned media, and can be done through:

- Social media advertising
- Influencer marketing
- Pay-per-click (PPC)

Putting funds behind PR content is becoming increasingly popular. Since the majority of social platforms are reducing organic reach for business accounts, it's a fantastic way to make sure your content gets in front of the people you want to see it.

Another part of the work of PR: Earned Media

This PR strategy that comes through word of mouth. Defined as the tactic to boost conversation around your brand to the target audience, there's a chance that you're already collecting earned media from your owned content.

But, earned media is the hardest type of PR strategy to execute. That's because you need to do something before you can get it. It takes a lot of effort and hard work — hence why it's "earned".

Having said that, earned media is the best tactic to build your reputation.

Let's face it: If you see your business, product, or services being:

- Reviewed on industry blogs
- Praised in customer testimonials on social media
- Ranked highly in a search engine

How is public relations different than advertising?

- It's Unpaid vs. Paid. Earned vs. Purchased. Credible vs. skeptical. Public relations tastes great, advertising is less filling.
- There's an old saying: "Advertising is what you pay for, publicity is what you pray for."
- Advertising is paid media; public relations is earned media. This means you engage in media contact to convince reporters or editors to write a positive story about you or your client, your candidate, brand or issue. It appears in the editorial section of the magazine, newspaper, TV station or website, rather than the "paid media" section where advertising messages appear. So your story has more credibility because it was independently verified by

a trusted third party, rather than purchased. Here's a good chart from an article in Forbes:

Advertising	Public Relations
Paid	Earned
Builds exposure	Builds trust
Audience is skeptical	Media gives third-party validation
Guaranteed placement	No guarantee, must persuade media
Complete creative control	Media controls final version
Ads are mostly visual	PR uses language
More expensive	Less expensive
"Buy this product"	"This is important"

What else do PR people do?

They tell the story of your brand/company:

- PR professionals are empowered with the task of growing, guiding, and managing the consumer/stakeholder perception of your brand/company and the message received about your brand by these groups. PR professionals aid the marketing and advertising campaigns by adding an extra layer of substance to the message received by the consumer through articles, press releases, statements, events and comment through the media.

- When you read a news article, hear a radio spot from a DJ or journalist, read about an event or new product in your local magazine or newspaper, the chances are there is a PR professional behind that interaction creating that angle and message and guiding the way you receive it.

- PR pros are your brand's voice brand in print, radio, TV and online; they create a rich history and story that they share through the media.

PR specialists shape the debate / manage crisis situations.

- Think of the hundreds of job losses made through downsizing. Large corporations are now relying largely on their PR teams to help them shape the debate, take the mostly negative spin away from the severe job loss and inform and guide the consumer to the truth and reasoning behind the redundancies. PR professionals in this case give a "voice" to the corporation and its decision and allow the consumer an insight into the minds of the company. They get two sides to the story, and hopefully balance the negative and positive.

- Generally, PR professionals aim to get the most accurate and positive news out to the consumer about their brand, but there is always an element of negative to be managed about any brand. How that is managed by the media and in turn interpreted by the consumer, is guided by the PR professionals. They:

They write, and write, and write.

- After identifying key messages and strategic direction for brand/company, PR professionals work out exactly what message, story, event, angle or news piece to deliver. Then... they write. Writing is a massive portion of the PR professionals' role. Writing fact sheets, news releases, media pitches, positioning statements, white papers, PowerPoint presentations, op-ed pieces, web copy, blog posts, ad copy, speeches and holding statements, event results and captions. Every single one of these methods offers just one more opportunity to shape and guide the message given to the public. You better love writing if you want to succeed in PR.

Plan events.

- Events are a wonderful way to unite a consumer, get the public to interact with your brand, and get the media involved. PR events range from an ice cream truck for the local community, to getting thousands of people and media to a politician's rally. These events are a further way to spread a positive message and sentiment about brands to the public, communicate news about a new product or story, and give the consumer news. The pre, during and post publicity for these events provide the PR professional with multiple touch points and ways to bring their view to the consumer.

Engage in media contact.

- PR professionals have to form strong relationships with media, developing media contact skills to pitch stories and angles to them on a daily basis. Usually this activity derives from targeted media lists. To reach a target audience, PR tools include developing as many angles as possible, and find reporters from as many beats as possible to cover their story. The most memorable and creative pitches result in positive coverage. Knowing media and having those relationships in place is one of the key measures of a successful PR professional. It requires constantly keep abreast of many types of media.

Find influencers.

- The best ambassador for your brand or organization is your consumer's best friend, idol or respected leader. If your friend tells you to use brand X over brand Y, you're likely to take their advice, right? Well, it's the same with PR. Finding and forming alliances with influencers who can share the brand/ company message in their own way, from their heart is far more effective than you telling them via a TV advert. Think Leonardo DiCaprio and Al Gore sharing their voice to **Live Earth**, or Hamish McDonald and Carrie Bickmore on **The Project** pushing for a cause, a brand they trust or an organization they believe in. You trust them; you listen...

Tell the truth.

- Sometimes, in the heat of the moment, it's tempting to skip steps, make assumptions, and push the button on a story before the facts are checked. Sometimes PR professionals are criticized for pushing the boundary of the truth just to get positive coverage for their company. Don't be tempted to take shortcuts that will undermine your credibility with your team, client, or employers. Tell the truth over the sake of a good story.

Educate themselves.

- PR professionals have one of the best jobs on the planet. Public relations professionals claimed the number 41 spot a recent list and it's easy to see why. They have to be articulate, well read, and intelligent. They need to understand and care deeply about the subject matter they represent to get anywhere. They have to keep up on current events, read the newspaper, and know about what's going on in the world. They have to be across their target market, get into the minds of the best business journalist and their public and work out how best to approach them.
- PR people are storytellers, creating narratives to advance their agenda. PR can be used to protect, enhance or build reputations through the media, social media, or self-

produced communications. A good PR practitioner will analyze the organization, find the positive messages and translate those messages into positive stories. When the news is bad, they can formulate the best response and mitigate the damage.

Part III

PR Tools: how to write a press release: 10 best news release tips for 2019

I don't care what anyone says – the news release is alive and well is one of the most important PR Tools. Here are some press release tips and my newest thinking in how to write a news release.

Its purpose is clear: inform the media. Provide greater exposure and credibility for your business. Add to SEO. If a magazine, newspaper, or online publication picks up your story, the benefits are enormous. Without a press release, there is no story.

Why is publicity so credible and so different from advertising? In an age of influencers and social media, let's remind ourselves that third-party (media or social platform) endorsements are alive and well, too. The general population is more likely to trust a third-party influential such as reviewer, columnist, or reporter. The believable third party delivers the information. In advertising the advertiser controls the message. Consumers know it's a paid advertisement and they may be skeptical of the claims being made.

To create a press release that catches the attention of a journalist here are some basic tips you should follow when writing your press release.

1. Use the correct press release format.

For a release to be taken seriously it must be easy to read. With all the correspondence editors receive, they usually to publish or not as a snap judgment. There are many acceptable formats. Even so, try these press release tips; They have worked for the PR Writer.

Brands are important. Highlight them in all releases. Include logos, taglines, and important identifying information like how to reach you so media can follow up – though it will be mostly you making the calls. Even dates are important, allowing editors to confirming that it's timely and check when it was released.

2. Press release headline tips: Grab their attention.

Write a strong, <u>attention-grabbing headline</u> in one line or less. The normal rules of grammar do not apply in headlines. Headlines must be compressed tightly. A classic example is Headless Body in Topless Bar. Notice there is no verb or words like the or an. Use strong powerful verbs. Study <u>tabloid newspaper headline style</u> and it's all explained there. Everything happens in life in 15 seconds – you can decide a mate or accept a news release – make those 15 seconds count in a headline.

3. How to write a press release: make sure your story is newsworthy

Before you begin, ask the following questions:

- Would anyone outside my organization care about this announcement?
- Is this story relevant AND interesting to my target audience?

If you have answered an honest 'yes' to these questions, then keep going. If not, put the press release away. Wait until there is something worthwhile to release. Otherwise, you lose credibility with journalists. They have been sent too many un newsworthy press releases.

4. More press release guideline tips: Include the date

Include the dateline. Tell the media where the press release comes from, or where your company is located. It's especially important for regional magazines or when announcing an event. The Associated Press Stylebook or similar Canadian Press version are the go-to guide how to write a news release.

Next is the lead and body of your press release. The lead, or first sentence, is just as crucial as the headline. It should also recap the headline; it is connected to the headline. In effect, the news in the headline must be found in the lead. It should be full of information and answer most, if not all, of the 5 Ws. (Who, what, when, where, why and how) It should leave your reader wanting more.

Journalism writing, short and to the point must be concise and without fluff. Keep it short; one page is usually more than enough. Save the creativity and humor for feature stories.

Use quotations to reinforce your main point.

Remember, a journalist may end up using your quote in their story word for word. Make sure it includes the release's main message and that it sounds like a real person. Think about it: does it sound like something that person would say? If quoting someone in your organization, person better know their stuff – and answer any media requests.

5. Make connecting easy.

It's usually good to end with your company's boilerplate statement. Every company should have a general boilerplate statement that describes the company. A few sentences that summarize the company's history and offerings can go along way if you use it consistently.

Again, be sure to include your contact information for follow-up. When sending your release to media representatives, it is usually best to copy and paste it into the message of an e-mail. Most editors will not open attachments from unknown sources.

6. Additional press release guidelines: Figure out who is most likely to pick up your story

Constantly changing, and shrinking terribly and sadly, the media landscape is difficult to keep up with and keep track of who is working (or not working) -- and where. Maintaining media lists and keeping up with all the media moves is nearly impossible. That's why a trustworthy media contact database that is constantly reviewed and updated is worth its weight in gold. There are a few companies like Cision that provide searchable data bases, But before picking one, make sure it includes the desirable regional, global or industry publications. Check how they ensure their information is up to date, although even in days of media stability that was almost always out of date.

7. Go beyond the wire

Your job isn't over once you've sent out a release on the wire. Reach out to a few of the journalists or influencers and send an email about your release -- paste your release into the email with a short summary. Include images or links to videos that provide more details, but no attachments. Files clogging inboxes won't win any friends.

8. Press Release format

Show you know who you're pitching, so press releases looks less like mass e-mails. Change up the subject line and first paragraph depending on what industry the magazine is targeting. The principle is:

Make it as easy for journalists in whatever you do. They must generate ideas and work rapidly; include other article/post ideas—just a headline and quick description and how you can help. Incorporate different viewpoints and products *in addition to your own.*

For a release to be worthwhile outside of just being company news, it must connect to larger trends happening globally. Connect your news to the bigger picture. Add value. How is this news is relevant beyond the release itself? What does it mean to customers and consumers?

9. Press Release Tips: story within the story

Find the story within the story. If you are giving a charitable donation highlight the charity and explain what it plans to do with the funds, explain and how it might make a difference. Include photos of the donation. Think in terms of providing a package of storytelling, quotes, and photos to make a reporter's life easy.

10. Tips for Writing a Press Release: research

Before writing the press release, research should be done on what the media has been covering in recent weeks or months. Re-angle your press release to discuss how your new product, service, or award is relevant to the issue. Remember that journalists don't care about your product or your company (unless you are an industry giant), so you have to make them understand the value of your press release in the context of the whole industry.

Coda

Proofread your press release — and make it grammatically flawless. Let some others read it as well — before sending it out. Even a single mistake can dissuade a reporter from taking it seriously.

If you'd like to more or I can help you, click on the <u>contact</u> page. I will respond right away.

Part IV

10 PR Tools for strengthening media relations

In this continuing perspective on PR tools, one of the most important and overlooked ones is how to build media relationships. If you consider what is a media relations strategy, then you understand the importance of how these tools pertain to many facets of life, including getting a job, team building and strengthening client relationships. These will be covered in successive posts. What is media relations – glad you asked. Here are 10 PR tools for building and succeeding with media contacts, seven essential pitch letter tips and 12 suggestions for making the pitch project more successful. (Or look at this classic Forbes story on how <u>NOT to write</u> a pitch letter).

Most important overall tip: getting to know media.

This always seems the most daunting, especially to younger PR professionals. There are two parts to this: the first is technical. Keeping track of the movements, shutdowns, transfers, closures, firings and general decimation of the conventional media. It's difficult to do this but once you do identify someone who can be helpful to your client or organization, set up <u>a Google alert</u>; it's not just for companies, it'll track people too. If you have become a media relations specialist, this is very useful in these troubled times for media.

In my <u>Chicago</u> days, there were certain bars where real journalists hung out – Billy Goat's, and O'Rourke's, for example. The social scene was vigorous and media relations often were of the intimate sort. However, that's a bygone day. Now there is dispersion among media survivors, not to mention overwork for those who are left.

But what about once someone is identified as a contact? Why are media relations important -- how do you get to know them? here are 10 important tips:

1. **The best way to understand media relations** is to follow what an individual does diligently. Get to know them as well as they know themselves. How do you do that?
2. **First, read everything the person** publishes, both in their home media and on all social assets. What does this accomplish?
3. **The best pitch** is an informed pitch.
4. **The media target is essentially** a stranger. But it's your job to get inside their heads. Being an expert on their writing and social comments develops a view into their minds. This in turn helps learning not only how to best pitch them, but also more importantly how to become a trusted source by helping them find other stories.
5. **People in the media**, frustrated and overworked, fatigued with PR pitches and phone calls, rarely have the chance to pursue the stories they'd like to cover, much less come up with ideas to find something original.

6. **They'd welcome someone** who understood their unique worldview, and coverage interests.

7. **It's not just topics** to write about but background information that will help the frazzled journalist add background, stimulate other ideas, or find out new facts they might not have considered previously.

8. **It's easy to say** there are too many journalists to engage in this kind of research. Your targets are way too numerous.

9. **Clearly, that's possible** but there is definitely a short list of those who can help you the most. And if it works out well, branch out to others.

10. **It is, however definitely** worth a try. It's been very successful for many PR pros, as a principal PR tool.

There are more tools for targeting media <u>here</u>.

Seven most essential pitch letter tips

Writing pitch letters is often considered a chore but are a necessity as a media relations specialist. They show the journalist what the story might look like, even though it's cast in PR terms. Few understand, however, that the pitch letter and the news release are interconnected and must reinforce each other. The pitch letter is the door opener, and the news release contains the news. Here are the seven tips.

1. **The subject line is like a headline.** As with news releases, make it punchy and memorable. It might be the only item read about the story. Don't just write one; create one and make it work. Especially if you are requesting attendance at a press event, give those writers or editors a really good reason to get up out of their chairs and get out of the office to attend your event.

2. **In the first paragraph tell journalists why the story is incredibly** compelling and what exactly what you want them to do. Come to an event, schedule an interview, review a product, with time and place it will occur. It's one of the most concise pieces of writing to be prepared. It also must comply with news basics, especially timeliness, roses in summer, earmuffs in winter.

3. **Use a first name with journalists.** Not Mr. or Ms. Too formal, A first name elevates the writer to their level, presenting you as a peer who is providing legitimate information needed to do their job. Personalize the rest of the story so the recipients feel it's aimed at them, not some giant horde.

4. **Use the second paragraph to illuminate the story.** What are the other details of the event or product that adds to its newsworthiness?

5. **The third paragraph is the what else** that either provides an additional angle. Who else will be there? What else might provide a reason to attend? In the last paragraph, set out the terms and conditions, such as is the invite transferable. If with a celebrity, is security involved?

6. **And then say when you will call** to follow up and do it!

7. **Last but not least**, make sure it's absolutely clear where to find you. Even though nine times out of ten, communicators are following up, sometimes the reporter does pick up the phone. If the idea is good enough.

The day then comes when the journalist answers the telephone and the PR pro launches into the pitch. There is an art to the pitch.

My Humber College students would often ask, what is the best order for pitching? Should you just call or what? My suggestions:

1. Send a pitch letter
2. Call but don't make reference to having sent a pitch.
3. More often than not, the reporters and editors, if they answer the phone, will say can you send me a pitch?
4. Never ever say, 'Hey, I already did.'
5. Have a news release ready to go if it's requested.

Now the day has come: the pitch says you will phone, and you do. And to your great surprise, the reporter answers the phone. Make sure you are cool, calm and collected and ready to pitch. The first question is always—how do I identify myself? Here are 12 tips to make it an easier process.

1. **Don't spend too much time** on explaining who you are by providing your full name and that of the agency and the client. By then you've lost them.
2. **Most scientific accounts** say that people can tell almost instantly whether they will like someone or not. Imagine you are sitting next to someone in a bar. Turn your head and you know. Immediately. Go or no go.
3. **The same with journalists**. If someone is fumbling and comes up with a whole long background about who they are, and the story still isn't clear, the moment is lost.
4. **Get to the story right away**. It's often called an elevator pitch. Can you describe the entire story in 15-20 seconds? It's the human time span for understanding new information. Practice is over and over until it's internalized, which leads to:
5. **NEVER read your pitch**. A huge turn off. Know the story and be natural. Think of it as talking to a friend.
6. **If the reaction isn't great,** be prepared with other angles.

7. **Listen carefully;** sometimes the reporter has accepted the idea and PR people are so busy pitching they don't pick it up.
8. **If it is accepted**, make sure you have all the assets to be provided at your fingertips. For example, know the times the spokesperson can talk to the reporter. Have a product sample and a means to deliver it if you are pitching a product.
9. **The trick question**, especially to new PR people, is who else are you pitching, i.e., competitors? Have an answer ready.
10. **The other trick question** is 'is it an exclusive.' While sometimes it is, avoid agreeing to that at all possible costs. It's just a form of bullying.
11. **While it's very depressing** to get 'no' for an answer, don't give up right away. At least ask why the pitch doesn't work, or what else you might do as a follow up.
12. For more help with your news release or pitch letter, <u>contact</u> The PR Writer.

The last word

Of Is and By is based on the idea that communications writing or media English is different from most other prose. Online writing and journalism should be brief and convey information concisely -- the aim of this writing system. Its basic tenets are simplicity, compression, plain language and rapid comprehension. Today, with short attention spans in the iPhone, Snapchat, Instagram and Twitter age, it's even more important to communicate the most information in the shortest time.

The communicator only receives the audience's attention momentarily; *Of Is and By* makes sure you don't lose the reader due to short attention spans. Shorten, prune, edit, and always eliminate unnecessary words: these are time-honoured lessons that the great E.B. White pioneered in the still worthwhile *Elements of Style*. If I can be terribly forward, I'd like to think that *Of is and By* is an update to that worthy text and hope you thought so too.

Congratulations! By reading this book, you have taken a big first step in becoming a better writer and improving communications everywhere. You will be the authority among your job, organization, company or media about how to apply these skills. The change will be fast and remarkable. For updates sign up at <u>The PR Writer</u>.

Section VI:
Additional readings

Chapter 23

A. How to become a better writer

Improving writing is like the old New York joke, where the tourist asks, "How do you get to Carnegie Hall?" and the street-smart Brooklynite says, "Practice!" There is no substitute for writing whatever you can, when you can. Treat every writing occasion as practice: don't let emails be less than excellent. They represent you as a brand. Malcolm Gladwell's 10,000-hours rule, as explained in his excellent Outliers, applies. Those who master their craft, from the Beatles playing nine hours a day in Hamburg dives to Bill Gates taking over his prep school's computer, must do so for at least 10,000 hours.

My own 10,000 hours happened at Chicago's legendary City News Bureau training ground where a reporter might write or accept dictation for 30-40 news stories in one day--from court cases to burglaries, robberies and murders to three-alarm fires, traffic jams and politics. Hearing experienced reporters dictate their stories was particularly instructive (see how the plural rule for eliminating gender works here, even though it was one reporter at a time). You also learned such fine distinctions as the difference between a burglar (breaks into premises) and robber (accosts you on the street).

Improving writing is less about mastering forms like the news release, pitch letter or memo and more about specific words and constructions used every day.

When I became a writing teacher, these ideas were refined at Humber College and Ryerson University, and in my @rotman-pr consulting firm. They resulted from many published articles, columns and blogs and experiences at the Washington Post, Metropolis magazine, Hill and Knowlton Inc., and Harshe-Rotman & Druck/Ruder Finn & Rotman Inc., and Bennington College, all places I have been grateful to be associated with. My father, Morris B. Rotman, a PR pioneer and legendary editor, taught me many of my first, memorable lessons. Learning languages, a passion of mine, has proven to unlock better writing skills more times than I can remember, as has observing really bad writing as it fruitlessly multiplies in careless copy, especially in paid PR newswires. In my writing classes, they are often shocked to learn they must erase much of what Academia teaches now that they must master media writing. Telling them about "Of, Is and By," however, appears to reduce blood pressure somewhat.

II. English, our basic tool

Let's talk about the English language. It's has taken over the world and is best for writing concisely. In fact, this system would not work in other familiar languages, like French.

Unique among major Western languages, English is a mongrel, a hybrid mix between Germanic Anglo-Saxon and Norman French. Vikings and the Scots, Irish and Welsh contributed many words to this lively stew. Julius Caesar and the Romans invaded the British Isles in 56 BC, gradually incorporating the wild tribes into the Roman Empire until withdrawing as Rome fell in the early years of the Common Era. Few are aware of this, as the Latin language did not conquer the region, as it did in France, Spain, Portugal or Italy; the Roman linguistic influence remains mostly in place names like Brittania and a road system with London at the centre. English offers grammatical flexibility along with its notable irregularity, the bane of non-native speakers attempting to learn it.

Our syntax remains resolutely Anglo-Saxon, a Germanic off-shoot, but as a result of William the Conqueror's 1066 Norman Invasion, Latin-derived French words, along with Greek, were incorporated, expanding the vocabulary greatly. (English maintains the world's largest vocabulary, with "Web 2.0" said to be its millionth word). In William's time, French became the Court language. Old English gave way to Chaucer's Middle English, and pronunciation changed (the Great Vowel Shift). All this led to Shakespeare and Modern English. The British Empire and the American rise to world power and economic dominance after World War II set English on its course to become the most important global language, if not its most widely spoken. By sheer numbers, the combined Chinese dialects are number one.

Anglo Saxon thankfully remains the heart and soul of English. Every day some of our favourite four-letter words come from Anglo-Saxon. I'd love to write them here but saying the F word will suffice. When aristocratic Norman French swamped peasant Anglo Saxon, words like copulate, defecate and urinate entered English in the place of the four letter words we know and love. It pleased me to no end in Frost/Nixon, Frank Langella's President Nixon character unnerves his interviewer, Michael Sheen's David Frost by asking, "Did you fornicate last night?" This marked the publicly puritanical (but privately profane) Nixon as a false high-minded Latinate thinker.

"The buck stops here," plain speaking (and Nixon-hating) President Harry Truman's formula for taking responsibility reveals Anglo Saxon simplicity at its best. (To Truman, Nixon was "a no good, lying bastard. He can lie out of both sides of his mouth at the same time...")

There is no doubt as to the 'buck stops here's meaning. Everyone can understand it. Truman was also famous for "If you can't stand the heat, get out of the kitchen" and for firing Gen. Douglas McArthur, notable for the simple, "I shall return," a promise he fulfilled to the beleaguered Filipinos in World War II. Another one like it is former Canadian Prime Minister Pierre Elliott Trudeau's famous statement "Just watch me," when asked "how far he'd go?" in combating the FLQ terrorists. (The next day he'd declare martial law by invoking The War Powers Act). The fluently bilingual Trudeau picked "just" from Middle English, with an original Latin origin but the whole phrase is just like Truman's. His son Justin also became PM, making a comment heard around the world when asked why his new cabinet was so diverse and gender-balanced, and he said: "Because it's 2015!" Ernest Hemingway, still my favourite writer, explained his method as: "My aim is to put down on paper what I see and what I feel in the best and simplest way." His use of simple, emotional language is still the gold standard: "Courage is grace under pressure."

Interestingly, mothers speak to children with a higher percentage of Anglo-Saxon verbs. They of course wouldn't say to Johnnie or Susie, "It's time to urinate," so we start life with short four-letter words The great style expert Fowler said the highest majority of good writing contains this vocabulary. Finally, the most emotional resonant words in our language come from Old English dear, daughter, death, doom." Why not use them in your own writing too? (See chapter on this subject).

III. How I Became a Language Maven

My earliest memories of a different language are a family trip to Cuba, which coincided with the advent of Castro's revolution, relevant now as that was the last time many Americans had been there. I remember trying to pick up words and learning to count at Veradero Beach. In Glencoe, Ill., where I grew up, an itinerant Spanish teacher, Señora Barrigos, came to class in elementary school, by walking from school to school; her perfume preceded her and it was a big joke among the students. This was prescient on the school's part as no one cared about bi-lingualism in the States at that time. As high school approached, my mother Sylvia S. Rotman, told me I'd be learning French, as it was 'somehow' important. It didn't have that much effect on me, although I had the same teacher, Mrs. Lawrence, all four years. She was in her 20s then; and in later years, my spouse and I had dinner with her and her husband, as we had some mutual friends. That was interesting.

During high school I fell in love with Hemingway. He was from a Chicago suburb, had gone off to war, entered journalism and tried to find the simplest way to convey stories and words. He even wrote for the Toronto Star. I went to see his boyhood homes in Oak Park and once went to an exhibit at a bookstore where all of his first editions were displayed and I remember all the books to this day. I have a few Hemingway firsts now but the person had every single one, even articles in long-vanished literary magazines. Later, not only did I go running with the bulls in Pamplona (featured in the Sun Also Rises) and lived for a while on the Left Bank in Paris, and tried to write where Hemingway sat with a pad and pencils he sharpened with a knife. I wrote a story about it, called the "Last Glass of Absinthe." Later Woody Allen wrote "Midnight In Paris" about the "Lost Generation" in Paris and he took the idea a lot further than I did, though my writing teacher at Bennington College, Bernard Malamud, liked my idea.

While I was doing the minimum in French class, I had started to work as a copy boy at the City News Bureau of Chicago, the legendary round-the-clock wire service that served as a non-union training ground for young journalists. The major newspapers, the Chicago Tribune and Sun-Times, owned it jointly. Anyone who was anyone in Chicago journalism started there. Every day I'd look at the editors mark-up copy and then transcribed dictated stories on the telephone. Reporters called in their stories from the scene and I'd transcribe them. Invaluable grounding in the reporter's art. I also had to enter stories into the teletype on weekends for distribution, again internalizing journalism style. Gradually I became a 'rewriteman' and wrote stories myself from reporter's notes. My father had worked at the City News Bureau before WWII and a bit after, before he became a PR pioneer. He tried to edit my school newspaper copy. His colleagues called him a 'legendary' wordsmith and had in fact edited a base newspaper during WWII.

But even then, it hadn't come together.

It took being in Spain and hearing Spanish and starting to pick it up easily. Then I realized I had a talent for languages. Hemingway could speak French or Spanish when he reported and I resolved to do that too. In short order, I studied Spanish, then Russian, took a summer course in Mandarin. While in PR, I took a pass at Portuguese and Italian and studied Japanese at the Japan-America Society. Now I am trying to master Hebrew. Most of these have been curiosities and I only can speak some things in them. But they have taught me so much about English. Foreign language study gives you an education that speaking your own language never provides-- what it can do and what it can't.

There's no substitute for writing, of course, and editing your own and other's stories. And I have done a lot of that, which led me to develop the "Of, Is and By" better writing system. But for some reason, I see improvements in copy that others don't and live with the firm belief that I can make almost anyone's copy better. I really believe I can. There are even editing opportunities in the New York Times!

Acknowledgements

By teaching PR writing and working in PR and Journalism, I uncovered numerous opportunities to create tighter, more concise content, realizing I possessed special skills to boil down and eliminate extra words. Somewhat to my surprise, I could improve virtually anyone's content, skilled pro or student by viewing it with 'Of Is and By,' which became a new, simplified writing system. And that's how this book began, as I saved writing samples to demonstrate it. Now that Better Writer is published (and thank you for reading it), here are some people I've always wanted to thank, and who made this possible. Ellen Greenblatt, my life partner, to whom I owe everything. Her love is life enhancing and her comments were invaluable and skillful. My son and daughter, Josh and Talia, for being there and being so loving and such exemplary offspring. Sister Betty for always being encouraging and a lifelong friend. Parents, Sylvia and Morry, a legendary editor, and both good readers. Much-missed brother Jesse, for growing up in the same room and teaching me about life. Rabbi John Moscowitz, for trading writing and keeping a literary flame alive, not to mention much spiritual guidance. Branding guru Michael Marchese, now also a Cannabis industry financier, helped in more ways than he could ever know, collaborating on numerous branding, design and writing projects. Everyone at City News Bureau of Chicago but especially Paul Zimbrakos and Jim Elsener (look up his excellent baseball novel The Last Road Trip), who read and commented on a Better Writer draft. Thanks also to Palm Springs friends Leon Pascucci and author Michael Craft of FlabberGassed fame, who took the time to edit and proof an earlier draft. Blair Moody at Metropolis and still a great friend. The Washington Post at Watergate's conclusion, enabling me to observe (and be chewed out by) the legendary executive editor Ben Bradlee as well as have an up-close look at Woodward and Bernstein, the never-to-be-equalled investigative reporters. My wonderful and much-loved alma mater, Bennington College, for accepting me and exposing me to Bernard Malamud, Nicholas Delbanco, Alan Cheuse, Stephen Sandy, Sam Schulman, Tom Erlanger, Ellen Lang and Susan Feldman. To great Glencoe friend David Rich for much writing talk, and New Trier best friends Teresa Lemon and Doug Studt and later-in-life best friend Steve Durchslag.

Thanks to all of you for taking this journey with me.

Richard Rotman
@rotmanprwriter

About the Author

Richard Rotman grew up in Glencoe, Illinois on Chicago's North Shore, and lives in Toronto. He has devoted his career to helping writers learn and improve. He is currently working as the PR Writer and Copy Doctor. In the last decade, he was a media studies professor at Humber College, Toronto, teaching PR writing, media relations and politics and public affairs. He also taught PR courses at Ryerson University. He began his journalism career at the legendary around-the-clock City News Bureau of Chicago wire service and was a National Staff writer at the Washington Post, editor and publisher of Metropolis magazine, Toronto, and a radio and TV movie critic in that city. In public relations, he was an owner and partner at Harshe-Rotman & Druck, Inc., later Ruder Finn & Rotman, Inc. Chicago and New York. He also served as director of health care at Hill and Knowlton, Toronto before starting his own consultancy. A widely published writer and PR columnist, he has a B.A. in Literature and Languages, Bennington College, VT., and M.A., Politics, Columbia University, NYC. His blog about improving writing and other PR topics can be found at *https://theprwriter.com.*

Made in the USA
Middletown, DE
14 September 2019